W9-AEO-538

50 Nifty Thrifty Upcycled Fashions

Centerville Library
Washington-Centerville Public Library
DISCARD
Centerville, Ohio

Sew Something from Nothing

CYNTHIA ANDERSON

STACKPOLE
BOOKS

0 11557 01470 9

Copyright © 2015 by Stackpole Books

Published by
STACKPOLE BOOKS
5067 Ritter Road
Mechanicsburg, PA 17055
www.stackpolebooks.com

All rights reserved, including the right to reproduce this book or portions thereof
in any form or by any means, electronic or mechanical, including recording or by
any information storage and retrieval system, without permission in writing from
the publisher. All inquiries should be addressed to Stackpole Books, 5067 Ritter
Road, Mechanicsburg, PA 17055.

Printed in the United States of America

10 9 8 7 6 5 4 3 2 1

First edition

Cover design by Wendy A. Reynolds
Photography by Tiffany Blackstone and Cynthia Anderson
Illustrations by Cynthia Anderson

Library of Congress Cataloging-in-Publication Data

Anderson, Cynthia (Seamstress)
    50 nifty thrifty upcycled fashions : sew something from nothing / Cynthia
Anderson. — First edition.
      pages cm
      ISBN 978-0-8117-1470-9
      1. Clothing and dress—Remaking. 2. Textile crafts. 3. Textile waste—Recycling.
I. Title. II. Title: Fifty nifty thrifty upcycled fashions.
TT550.A53   2015
646.4—dc23
                                                            2015011116

Contents

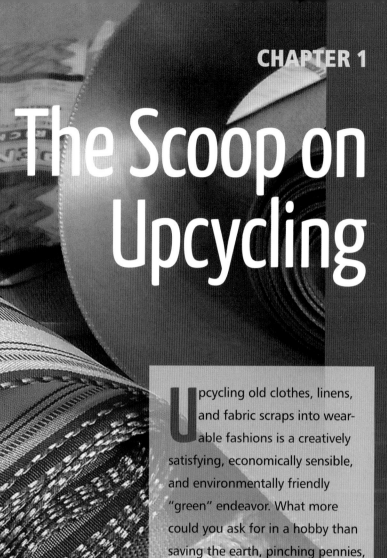

CHAPTER 1

The Scoop on Upcycling

Upcycling old clothes, linens, and fabric scraps into wearable fashions is a creatively satisfying, economically sensible, and environmentally friendly "green" endeavor. What more could you ask for in a hobby than saving the earth, pinching pennies, and tapping into your creativity all at the same time? Join the green club and choose to upcycle old clothing, linens, and fabric while releasing and fostering your inner creativity!

Upcycling 101

What is Upcycling?

Upcycling is the process of taking things you would throw away and making them into something useful without negatively impacting the environment. It is different from recycling in that it makes good use of limited resources, saves the energy costs and climate impact of recycling, and stretches your creativity. Upcycling old clothing is not just creating wearable art, it is designing and producing actual wearable clothing as well. It is a way for the artist to express inner creativity in a practical, yet whimsical way.

Why Go Green?

Do you have a clue how much clothing goes to the landfill every year? According to the EPA, 85 percent of unwanted clothing is discarded and accounts for more than 4 percent of municipal solid waste volume. The EPA Office of Solid Waste reports that Americans throw away more than sixty-eight pounds of clothing and textiles per person per year. In 2005 the volume of discarded clothing in the United States was eight million tons. It has continued to increase since then.

Stop throwing it away right now! Extend the life of out-of-style, ill-fitting fashions by refashioning them. Give your old clothes a second chance. Even if the label says dry clean only, wash and dry it and redesign it into something more practical, stylish, and usable.

Essence of Thrift

Upcycling is a way of life that honors thrift. It is based on a triage of spending that is the essence of thrift. Start by using what you have and move up from there.

    Buy
    Make
    Thrift
    Swap
    Borrow
    Use what you have

Make Something from Nothing

You'll spend less and leave a smaller carbon footprint by making something of greater value out of something you either already own or can buy at the thrift store for next to nothing. Six or eight worn T-shirts cut and sewn together make a smashing new wraparound skirt (see page 30) with very little effort. Some out-of-style, slightly shabby silk blouses can have a new life as a tunic like the Silky Stripper on page 92—guaranteed to turn heads! Just because the moths have feasted on some sweaters doesn't mean they can't have a stunning new life as a dress like the Patchwork Sweater Dress on page 52.

Upcycling allows you to incorporate into your projects bits and bobs and pieces of history as tangible symbols of family heritage. A button from great-grandfather's WWII uniform, pockets made from dad's silk graduation tie, or a piece of lace from mother's wedding dress—it is so satisfying to tuck a family memento into an upcycled work of art!

Wabi Sabi

Wabi Sabi is a Japanese aesthetic that embraces the nature of the impermanent, of imperfection and the transient. It honors finding beauty in nature and accepting that there is a natural progression of growth, decay, and death. Wabi Sabi embraces that which is aged, worn, and shows the wages of time and wear. Wabi Sabi would be shopping at thrift stores and flea markets, not shopping at the mall. Keep this concept in mind as you work on these upcycling projects. None will be perfect and none will last forever. Things you upcycle won't be perfectly symmetrical, they won't be permanent, and they won't be costly. They *will* be ingenious and stylish, and will give you great personal satisfaction.

Basic Materials and Equipment

Best Sources for Upcycling Fodder

First of all, you need old or unwanted clothes to work with: old sweaters, dresses, suit coats, dress shirts, and so on. You'll also want a stock of table linens, handkerchiefs, dresser scarves, pillowcases, and other old fabric items, both to use in the projects in Chapters 7 and 8 and as sources for gorgeous old embroidery, lace trims, and fabric scraps for linings. Almost any castoff item can be used in some way!

Your family's closets are the first best source for items to upcycle. Of course, giving unwanted or outgrown clothing to a friend or charity thrift store is another way to clear out your closet. But many items aren't suitable for this use. Set aside items that are:

- stained
- too worn
- torn or moth-eaten
- too warm or too cool for your climate
- seriously outdated

Such items will bring no value to the resale shop, and would likely just end up in the landfill anyway. But you can give them new value by creating something fabulous out of them.

After you raid your own and your family's and friends' closets for unwanted items, try the following sources for more upcycling fodder:

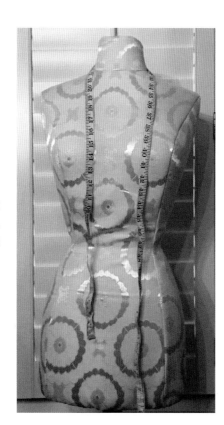

- thrift stores
- clothing exchanges
- resale/consignment shops
- lost and found departments
- yard sales, estate sales, tag sales, and garage sales

You could even form a small group of fashion upcyclers and trade among yourselves! You'll find cheap materials to craft with as well as reducing the amount of solid waste going to landfills.

Preparing the Fabrics for Production

Always wash your found clothing and linens before you upcycle them. Sometimes the item is so old and so fragile that it disintegrates as you wash it. While this is heartbreaking, it is better to know it can't be used *before* you have invested time and energy in transforming it into something new.

Exceptions to the wash-first rule might be centuries-old textiles or fabrics that you can see are already shredding without touching the water. These fabrics aren't a good choice for projects that will be worn regularly, but if you are making an item that will be used on one occasion—such as a bride's dress—and then saved as an heirloom, working a piece of fragile antique textile into a project works great.

Wash the cottons and linens by hand. Presoak them in a chlorine-free spot remover to get rid of as many stains as possible.

To felt wool sweaters, machine-wash them in color groups and dry them in the dryer. If you have just one sweater to felt, you can boil it in a big pot on the stove, stirring frequently and vigorously until it is felted as much as you want. Store the felted sweaters by color in big plastic tubs or self-closing bags.

If you like, you can dye your sweaters and fabrics to get custom colors; this is an art in itself. I recommend you start your dyeing experiments on smaller projects, trying different methods, including eco-dyeing. Take a class, read some related blogs, and study online tutorials to learn more about dyeing fabric.

Basic Equipment

A sewing machine—nothing fancy—is necessary for this upcycling adventure. There are parts of the projects you can do by hand-sewing but a sewing machine will serve you well for long seams. You will also need pins, thread, safety pins, an iron and ironing board, pressing cloth (a nice soft tea towel works fine), scissors, and a rotary cutter and mat for several projects. A stash of notions, buttons, and ribbons will provide you the tools you need to upcycle clothing and linens.

Notions

Elastic

You can always use more elastic, in any width. Never pass it by if the price is right. You can also scavenge it from clothes you're upcycling: cut the elastic off worn-out or outgrown pants, skirts, and undies that still have good elastic waistbands.

Seam Binding

Never pass up a packet or two of seam binding or seam tape at a good price at a tag sale. If it is in its original packaging and the price says 15¢, you have scored some fine vintage seam binding. There are a million ways to use seam tape. Use it like ribbon or for contrasting trim. Loop the tape and tack it every few inches around a hemline to make a lovely loopy edge trim on a jacket. Rip the rayon hem tape in half lengthwise to make imperfect, frayed ribbons for trimming (as seen in the slip dress Faith on page 110). Use stretch lace seam tape anywhere you would use a ribbon. Because of its delicate look, it is perfect to use with other more solid ribbons. Single-fold and double-fold bias trim comes in many colors and widths. Be sure to factor in the weight of the fabric when using a binding.

Buttons

A recycler can never have too many buttons. They are so versatile. They can be used to trim a neckline (like the Tribal Tunic on page 94), to embellish bodices (like the slip dress Hope on page 113), or to add interest to a jacket front (like *Le Smoking* on page 74)—the sky's the limit! Sort out the shank-back buttons from the flat buttons with holes. Shank-back buttons also make great jewelry. Then sort the buttons by color and store them in one of those fish tackle storage boxes.

Rickrack

Ribbons

While rickrack is still being produced today, there is nothing so colorful as the vintage rickrack from back in the day. It is guaranteed to show up at estate, tag, and yard sales. Take it home and use it up! What could be prettier than the little edge of colorful rickrack peeping out past the edge of a hemline as on the Tuscan Rose Tunic on page 133. Don't scrimp on the rickrack.

Can an upcycler have too many ribbons? Impossible! Save the ribbon or cloth tape from every single package you ever receive and store it in plastic bags by color. When working on a purple project, pull out your purple ribbon stash and keep it handy. Use it for bows, for straps, for belts, or for flowers. The greater the variety of textures and shades you add to a project, the more it comes to life. Think of Monet's *Water Lilies* with only one color of lily— *jamais*! Don't even think of putting a strip of ribbon in the trash—upcycle it!

Tulle

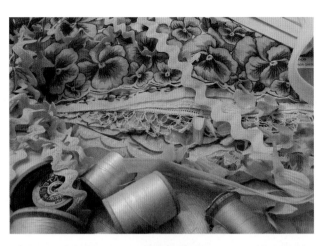

Rolls of tulle are a staple for upcycling women's fashions. Collect them in all colors, especially when you find them for 50 percent off or at a garage sale. A little tulle under the hemline of a dress can add body and flair (like in the Little Black Dress on page 56). Tufts of tulle can add just the right *je ne sais quoi* to a spectacular piece like Lavender's Blue on page 87. Check out the remnant rack for remnants of tulle in colors you love. Often a little piece of tulle is just what is needed (like on the slip dress Faith on page 110)!

Vintage Notions

Never pass a garage or yard sale without checking for sewing notions. Be a vintage notions scavenger. Every household has them, and few shoppers need more. The vintage colors are amazing. Bias tape, lace hem tape, rick-rack, zippers—they can all make splendid embellishments for a green project. Use it up. Enjoy it. Don't hoard it!

Designing Tips

You may not think of yourself as a fashion designer but you could be—I promise. Here are some tips.

Love Art

Think about the art that you love. What forms of media art and artists speak to you? Mosaics? Colorists? You can pay homage to them when upcycling. If your favorite artist is Mark Rothko, cut and paste a few shots of his paintings in your journal. When you are ready to design an upcycled project, look at your Rothko pictures and choose a color scheme. Josef Albers and his color-blocking method will help you as you choose the colors of sweaters you want to use, like the orange sweater on page 48. Take a note from the Impressionists (the roses on *Le Smoking*) and try some ways to make a print fabric softer and less precise. There will be no teacher grading you on your projects so take some chances. Let your favorite artists and favorite art styles guide you. Don't be shy about your designs. Follow your heart.

Watch the Runways

The ideas for the Wool Coat on page 78 came from Dolce & Gabbana. Coco Chanel inspired the Jackie Oh! jackets and the White Cashmere Sweater. Follow some upcycling blogs like Fashionista. Watch for ideas on Crush Cul de Sac. Follow the fashion houses that you love the most. Make yourself a board on Pinterest and pin the latest fashions from Chanel, Dolce & Gabbana, Valentino, Ralph Lauren. Study what you love about those designs, and then try out some of those ideas on your refashioning.

Deconstructing

A huge part of upcycling fashions reflects the trend of deconstruction fashion. Raw edges, zippers that show, fraying seams and hems, crazy seams that show—they are all components of the deconstructed look. This look is a made-in-heaven match for upcycling. Why spend hours hand-stitching a perfect invisible hem when cutting a raw edge hem for an already used skirt is way trendier and makes sewing so much easier. Remember that Wabi Sabi aesthetic.

Scarlett and the Curtains

Who could forget plucky Miss Scarlett making a beautiful dress from the drawing room curtains? There is a certain feeling of accomplishment, of adventure, of self-confidence that comes from making something from nothing. You don't need to go to the pricey fabric store and buy expensive fabric that you are afraid to cut into. You don't need to buy a costly pattern that looks too hard for your skill level. Just spend $10 at the thrift shop and come home and use your imagination. You can do this, Miss Scarlett! Put on your big girl pumps, and let's get it done.

Book Arrangement

This book is arranged by what each project started with—what the fashions or linens or fabrics were before they were upcycled—not what it turned into. Each chapter shows what you can do with a certain category of clothing or linens. What can you make from menswear? From lingerie? From sweaters? Read along and see.

Making Embellishments

The projects in this book use many different cloth flowers and other trimmings. Here are the directions for making some favorites—but there are many other possibilities. Look online for more tutorials and inspiration for other creative upcycled embellishments. Lacing a corset with a surplus dog leash as in the Violet Doily Delight on page 120 can work great, for instance. Your imagination is the only limit!

Chanel-inspired Camellia

This flower is lovely but not easy to make. You will need:

- Scraps of silk and silky fabrics
- 2" circle of felt in coordinating color
- 1" pin back
- Large cotton ball
- Round metal tablespoon and teaspoon measuring spoons
- Candle and matches
- Needle and thread
- Liquid fabric stabilizer
- Sponge brush
- Tweezers

Cut twelve to fifteen petal shapes from the silk/silky fabric. Cut half of them about 2" tall and the other half about 1½" tall. Gather three or four tiny tucks in the pointed end of each petal and stitch those tucks in place on the sewing machine.

Cut one 2–2½" circle of silk. Stitch around the circle and pull the threads to make it into a puff—this is the center of the camellia. Put the cotton ball inside the puff and sew it shut.

One by one, take each petal and place it right side down in the tablespoon. Using the sponge brush, coat the underside of the petal with fabric stabilizer. (I didn't have any fabric stabilizer so I just used a water-based glue/sealer in matte finish.) Place the teaspoon down into the tablespoon to trap the petal in a cupped shape. Hold the spoons over the heat from the flame of the candle and heat it for a while. Using tweezers, lift the petal out of the tablespoon. If the petal holds its spoon shape, carefully set it aside and start on the next one. If it does not hold its shape, put it back in and reheat. Repeat until all the petals are shaped and dry.

Choose three small petals and cluster them around the silk ball you made. Stitch them in place around the ball to form the bud center of the camellia.

Cut a 2" diameter circle from the felt. Place the pointed end of each large petal around the perimeter of the circle so the points meet in the center. Stitch the petals to the felt circle. Now place the smaller petals inside the circle of the larger petals so that they fill the gaps of the outer ring, and stitch them in place.

Place two or three small petals around the center bud that you have made and hand-stitch them in place. Place the whole bud section in the center of the felt circle and hand-stitch it in place. It should now be a beautiful camellia! Sew a pin back on it and enjoy. You can see a finished camellia on the Silky Stripper on page 92.

Felted Flowers

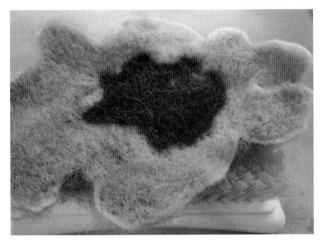

You will need:

- Scraps of regular lightweight craft store felt
- Chalk
- Wool roving
- Felting needles and felting sponge
- Patterns for flowers
- Card stock from junk mail

On the card stock, draw patterns for the flower shapes you want to make into felt flowers. Cut the patterns apart if the flowers have more than one color on them. Draw around the different flower component shapes with chalk on the lightweight felt, then cut them out. If the flower is all one color, pull some short pieces from the wool roving, spread the fibers apart, and lay them over the felt flower. Make one layer of roving, and then place a second layer of roving perpendicular to the first layer. Place the felt flower on the sponge and "felt" the roving into the flower until it looks the way you want it to. If the flower will be more than one color, protect the sections you are not working on by pinning the flower pattern over those sections. Felt the exposed section, then cover it with the pattern and felt the next section, and so on.

Once all the flowers are felted, you will use the same technique to felt them to the garment. Pin the flowers in place on the coat to make a pleasing pattern. Flower by flower, put the felting sponge under the coat where the flower is and use the felting needle to felt the flower to the body of the coat. See these felted flowers on the Wool Coat on page 78.

Frankenstein Flowers

These Frankenstein flowers are easy-peasy to make. All you need to make them is:

- Assorted silk flowers
- Tiny silk flowers for centers

Deconstruct a variety of silk flowers. Make new flowers by selecting three sizes of deconstructed flower blossoms and stacking them together for an entirely new species. Choose a tiny store-bought rose for the center and tack the new flower together. Tack the flowers to the project you are creating. See these on the Three-Hankie Top on page 130.

Gossamer Flower Headband

To make these flower-adorned accessories you will need:

- Scraps of organza in three shades of ivory (or color of your choice)
- Tiny pearl beads
- Plastic headband
- Scraps of silky ivory (or matching) lining
- Fray Check™ or similar product
- Paper, pencil, and scissors
- Hot glue gun and glue sticks
- Needle and thread

Start by ripping a strip of silky lining fabric about 1" wide and about a yard long. Heat up your glue gun and put a little glue on both sides of one end of the headband. Hold the strip of fabric so that you cover that end of the

headband, and then start wrapping the strip around and around the headband. Continue gluing and wrapping 2" at a time until you get to the other end of the headband. Finish off that end, making sure to cover the plastic and make a smooth end. Since both edges of the fabric are raw, dab the Fray Check™ on the raw edges so that your headband won't get shaggy later. Set the headband aside.

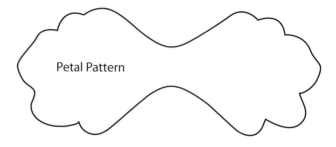

Petal Pattern

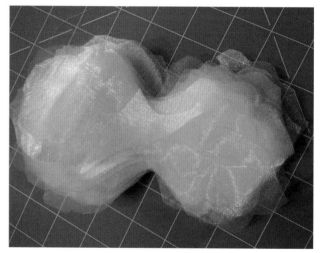

Draw a simple pattern for petals for your flower. This flower's petals were $6^1/_2$" long, $2^1/_2$" wide at the widest spot, and 1" wide at the narrowest part. For each flower cut out six petals, two from each shade of your color. Place each of the six petals in a cross shape as you stack them. Tack the stack of six petals together by hand or machine. Thread the needle and sew five tiny pearl beads in the center of the flower. Hand-stitch two of these flowers to the headband to the side of center. Take care to get the flower sewn down tightly to the headband. See this headband with the Duvet Bride's Dress on page 140.

Hosey-Posy

Items needed are:

- 2 pairs of pantyhose
- 2" circle of beige felt
- Sheer ivory ribbon—12"
- Scrap of tulle
- Button
- Candle, matches, and tweezers

Cut the petal-shaped crotch out of two pairs of pantyhose. Overlap one end of each of the petal shapes and tack them to the center of the felt circle, beige side up. Fold a 3" square of tulle into quarters. Take the tulle square to the sewing machine and place one end of the sheer ribbon in the center of the tulle square. Start stitching the ribbon onto the tulle in a circular manner, folding the ribbon over and over as you stitch out from the center. Cover the base tulle with the ribbon and cut off any spare ribbon. Cut three 3" squares of pantyhose. Using tweezers, hold the edges of the squares over the lighted candle so that the heat curls up the edges. Stack the three squares of pantyhose, place them on the center of the felt circle, and tack them down. Place the ribbon rose in the center of this stack and place the button in the very center. Sew the button down through the whole rose. Tack this Hosey Posy in the center back of the frock, where the bodice meets the skirt. See this flower on Knee High to Downton Abbey on page 102.

La Vie en Rose

You will need:

- Scraps of black silky fabric
- Scraps of black tulle
- 1" pin back
- 3" circle of black felt
- Candle, matches, and tweezers

Start with a large silky wedge about 4" wide at the widest point, 2" at the narrowest, and 26" long. Rip or cut three other 2"-wide strips from three other silky fabrics. Cut one 26" long and the other two 12" long. Sew a line of basting along one long side of each of the four strips. Pull the basting threads to cause the strips to ruffle slightly. Sew the widest strip in a circle around the felt circle. Sew each of the other strips in concentric circles to make three more rows of "petals" for the flower.

Cut two 6" circles of tulle and two 3" circles of tulle. Using the tweezers, hold the tulle circles over the heat from the candle until the edges draw up and melt together. Lay the large rose you have made onto the larger tulle circle. Lay the smaller tulle circle in the center of the rose. Tack them all together, and then sew the pin back onto the back. See this charmer on Paris in the Rain on page 150.

Round Doily Flower

These items are needed for this flower:

- Small lace doily, 2¹/₂" diameter
- 8–9" strips of assorted colors of beige and brown lace hem tape

To make this easy little flower, take one small lace doily, fold it in half, and then fold it in half again. Stitch the apex of the triangle together. Cut several strips of seam tape lace about 18–28" long. Rip some of them in half lengthwise to make them more ethereal. Lay out the strips in a pile with a common center, and then pick them up and tie a knot in them in the center. Tack the knot down to the back of the flower to form streamers for the flower. Tack this flower and its streamers to the garment at the center front of the skirt where the two dresser scarves meet. See this doily flower on the center front of Knee High to Downton Abbey on page 102.

Scrap Dragons

These far-out flowers are fun to make, and even more fun to wear—especially if you like a more spontaneous, less controlled look. To make one you will need:

- Scraps of fabric in several shades of a color group
- 3" circle of felt in similar color
- 1" pin back

Gather scraps of fabric in a wide range of shades of one color. The one on the Fortuny-style Cloak was made from four different pieces of home decorating sample scraps. Just cut the fabric samples in bands ranging from 1¹/₂" to 2¹/₂" wide and as long as your sample piece is. (My velvet pieces were only 9" long.) Use the widest strips on the outside first layer and then narrower strips as you work toward the center. I used the silky layer first, then the heavier silk tapestry, and finally the two velvets.

Run basting stitches in the silky fabrics and pull the thread so that they are ruffled. The velvet is too heavy to ruffle so use a seam ripper to poke little tucks in the velvet as you stitch.

Starting at the outside edge of the circle, begin sewing one end of each gathered strip to the felt using a zigzag stitch. As one strip is sewn down, pick up a strip of a different fabric and continue sewing the ends of the strips to the felt in concentric circles. As you get near the center, it will be more difficult to manage. I filled the center with a tiny circle about 2¹/₂" wide. I hand-stitched around the circumference of this little circle and pulled the basting stitches to make a tiny puff ball of the velvet. I stitched it down by hand in the center of the scrap dragon.

To make it shaggy, use small sharp scissors and cut each row of ruffles from the raw edge to just short of the center. Pull a little on each raw edge as you cut the petals so they will be nice and hairy. Sew a pin back on it and wear it on many different things.

See one of these shaggy splendors on the Fortuny-style Cloak on page 96 and smaller versions on the Jackie Oh, Oh jacket on page 72 and on Lavender's Blue on page 87.

Shaggy Lining Rose

These lovely flowers are easy to make and are a great way to recycle the lining of a jacket sleeve or pant leg. You will need:

- 6" diameter circle of double-thickness tulle for the flower base
- Some sleeve or pant leg linings cut into 2" or 2¹/₂" bands
- 2 or 3 wedge-shaped fabric scraps for leaves
- Knit scrap from the base dress
- Pin back (optional)

Cut a 2" or 2¹/₂" band from a sleeve or pant leg lining, leaving the side seams intact. Run a basting stitch along one side of the fabric strip and then pull the thread to gather it slightly. Sew the gathered band down about 3–4" in from the outside edge of the 6" tulle circle. Sew basting stitches down the center of a rectangular strip of lining fabric and gather it up. Coil this up and stitch it down to the center of this flower to fill it in.

Fringe the raw edge of the outer band of lining in the flower. Continue to pull threads until the rose is as shaggy as you would like.

Make some nice wedge-shaped leaves by sewing down the center of a wedge of fabric from the point right down the center. Pull the thread to gather each one up a little to make ruching. Sew these leaves under the rose or directly to the garment. Tack the rose directly onto the project or sew on a pin back if you want to use it as accessory pin. See one of these on the Little Black Dress on page 56.

Shaggy Stalactites

All you need are:

- Scraps of silky fabrics
- Scraps of lacy fabrics

Simply cut or tear wedges of silky fabrics and lace to make strips in a variety of lengths. Leave all edges raw. Sew them to the raw edges of skirt panels to make a sort of fringed edge to the panels. They can be used anywhere you want to soften the edges of a project or make borders without lines. Leonardo da Vinci called the technique *sfumato*; we call it softening the edges. See examples on the Faith Ivory Slip Dress on page 110.

For a variation on the shaggy stalactites, stitch down the center of a few of them with a long stitch, and then pull the thread to gather them up a bit. Be sure to follow up by restitching down the center with a shorter stitch so they do not come ungathered. You can see a few of these on the Faith Ivory Slip Dress as well.

Silky, Lacy, Pearly Flowers

These are easy to make. You will need:

- Silky and lacy fabrics
- Petals from ready-made silk flowers
- Pearl beads and buttons

Start by cutting an odd number of circles in descending sizes from your fabrics and pulling the petals off some white silk flowers. For example, for a three-layer flower, you could cut a 2$1/2$" circle, a 2" circle, and a 1$1/2$" circle. Once your circles are cut, stack them up, alternating with petals from the silk flowers, and sew them together, stitching a pearl bead or button to the center of the stack. You can make these flowers in any size by cutting the circles indifferent sizes. Make them as dense as you want by adding more petals in the stack. See one of these on the back bodice of the Hope White Slip Dress on page 113.

Silky or Knit Leaves

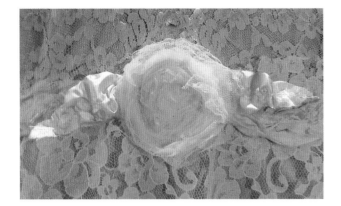

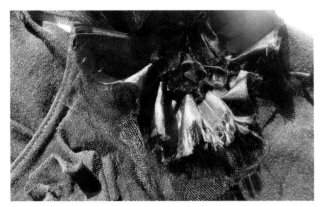

All you need are:

- 2 small scraps of silky or knit fabric

To make the leaves for a flower, all you need are two wedge-shaped pieces of fabric. Stitch down the center of the wedges with a long stitch, and then pull the thread to cause the leaf to draw up in size. See these leaves on the bodice of the Faith Ivory Slip Dress on page 110 and as knit leaves on the LBD on page 56.

Silky Sashes

All you need are:

- Scraps of silky fabrics
- Scraps of lacy fabrics

Start with two 3"-wide strips of silky fabric, each about 36" long. One will be the right sash, the other will be the left sash. Here I have embellished one side of each of the sashes. Leave the edges raw on both sash strips. Start at the large end of each and stitch down scraps of other silk fabrics and laces to build strength and texture into the sashes. The stitching lines reinforce and strengthen the sashes so they can bear being tied. The ones on the Faith the Ivory Slip Dress on page 110 are strengthened on one side only. If you like, you can sew scraps on both sides of the sashes.

Stringy Flower

These are very simple to make, requiring only two items:

- Scraps of felted wool sweaters
- Pin back

Start with twelve narrow wedges of felted wool in lengths from 3" to 7½" long and 1" wide or less at the wide end. Bundle them together at the wide ends and stitch them together. Add two wedges of green wool to form two leaves. Sew the leaves to the flower, and then sew the flower to a pin back. See this flower with the Orange Juju tunic on page 45.

Tulle Leaves

Materials needed are:

- Tulle scraps
- Candle, matches, and tweezers

Cut a leaf shape from tulle. The size should be in proportion to the size of the flower that needs leaves. Using the tweezers, hold the leaf over the lighted candle flame. (Don't put the tulle in the flame, but hold it above, just enough that it melts the edges of the leaf.) Sewing these leaves over leaves made of printed fabric softens the edges and blurs the lines, making the creation seem softer. See these on *Le Smoking* on page 74.

Tulle Roses

These ethereal beauties are easy to make and lend a big whammy to the design of your project. Craft stores offer inexpensive rolls of tulle in a variety of colors. You will need:

• Roll of 6" tulle

For each rose, cut a 6" square of tulle, and then fold that square into a 3" square. That is the base of your tulle rose. Cut an 18" to 24" length of tulle for each rose; fold the tulle in half or thirds and place the end of the strip at the center of the square. Begin stitching the tulle down in a spiral, folding the tulle over every couple of inches so that you are building a lovely round 3" rose. See one of these on the Faith Ivory Slip Dress on page 110.

Tulle Tufts

Cut tulle strips from about 6" to 12" long. Singe the edges of the strips using the candle and tweezers method. Once the edges are melted, pinch the center of your strip and tack the pinch with the sewing machine. The other method is to tie a knot in the center of the strip. This makes a little tuft of tulle to tuck between ruffles on a skirt. See these on the skirt of Lavender's Blue on page 87.

Tulle Whimsies

Items needed are:

• Tulle scraps
• Candle, matches, and tweezers
• Fabric glue

These little wisps of tulle can give your project a more Impressionistic impression, add a little fullness, or provide texture. Cut scraps of tulle into circles, leaves, or whatever shapes you desire. Using tweezers, hold the tulle shape over the heat above the candle flame until the edges of the shape curl. Sew whimsies down by hand wherever you want them, or put a dab of fabric glue down on the fabric and carefully place the whimsy in the glue until it sticks there. See these tulle whimsies on the bodice of the Hope White Slip Dress on page 113 and on the roses and leaves on the shoulder of *Le Smoking* Jacket on page 74.

Wooly Amoeba Roses

These look fab on woolen projects, and they are so easy to assemble! Items needed are:

- Scraps from wool sweaters
- Tulle
- Candle, matches, and tweezers
- Scraps of silky lining
- Buttons

To make the three wooly roses on the back of the Chic Stroller on page 65, I used three or four different colors of sweater scraps for each rose, plus silky lining scraps and tulle.

For each rose, cut three different colors of wool sweater into amoeba shapes in small, medium, and large sizes. Nest those onto an even larger amoeba shape cut from the silky lining fabric.

Cut two still larger amoeba shapes from the roll of tulle. Fire up the candle and use the tweezers to hold the tulle amoebas and melt their edges; you want to make the tulle misshapen, holey, and tattered. The two layers of tattered tulle go under the whole thing. Stack the other amoebas on top, tack them all together in the center, and sew buttons over the spot where they are tacked.

The two roses on the ends of the design each wanted leaves. Cut two leaf shapes from another sweater, tuck them in between the tulle layer and the lining layer, and sew them down. Arrange them in place and hand-sew them onto your garment.

CHAPTER 2

Upcycling T-Shirts and Blouses

o your T-shirts and blouses multiply overnight in your closets and dressers? Do you resist letting go of your favorite T-shirts, even after they are stained, shrunken, and worn out? Worry not. There is new life ahead for some oldies but goodies in your T-shirt and blouse department. Sail away on Swan Lake or make a Wabi Sabi statement with a skirt like Pierced Navel.

Helter-Skelter Blouse

A sleeveless blouse in summer is so versatile. Find one at the thrift store, or cut the sleeves out of one you no longer wear, and have a little creative fun jazzing it up. Ask around for some bits of crochet, dig in the button box, evoke your creative spirit, and you have a project that can be done in a flash with very few sewing skills. You don't even need a sewing machine for this creation, so try a little helter-skelter!

Materials

- Sleeveless blouse
- Assorted doilies and buttons
- Yo-yos from calico (Yo-yos are small gathered circles used in quilting.)
- Hankie scraps
- Crocheted hot pad
- Rickrack
- Scraps of fabrics in similar colors

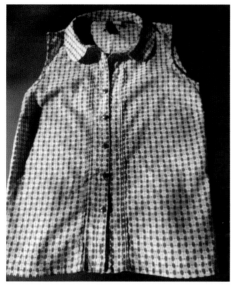

Preparations

This project starts with a basic sleeveless blouse. Gather doilies, calico yo-yos, hankie scraps, rickrack, and a crocheted hot pad for a pocket. Lay out the blouse on a flat surface. Audition the things that you have collected by pinning them in place on the front of the blouse.

Pin the hot pad pocket in place on one side of the lower front. For balance, pin a doily "vase" on the opposite lower front; add a doily and two yo-yos above the vase. Pin a larger doily over the wearer's heart and a piece of a hankie over the opposite shoulder. Balance it all out with smaller scraps and crocheted flowers.

Sewing

The only sewing on this shirt is for embellishment.

Embellishment

Once you are satisfied with the placement of the items, machine stitch them in place. Ice the cake by adding button centers to some of the flowers and rickrack stems to the flowers. Add rickrack to the collar, if you like, by placing it on the underside and topstitching it in place.

Tips

- This project can be done without regard to color groups if you are more inclined to like the helter-skelter look.
- Bet your granny has a lonely yo-yo or two that she would love to contribute to the cause!

Swan Lake Tunic

Wild and crazy hand needle-work just makes me smile! Why not get that vintage handwork out of tissue paper and sew it up into something wearable. The traditional black-and-white stripe is a nice counterpoint to the colorful mix of the skirt components. Dig out your quirky finds and incorporate them into something stylin'!

Materials

- Black-and-white striped T-shirt
- Embroidered satin panel, about 17" x 33"
- Woman's shirt for rectangular panel, about 18" x 57"
- Fabric scrap for rectangular panel about 18" x 48"
- T-shirt parts
- Decorative pin
- Chalk

Preparation

Wash, dry, and press the components. Draw four arches on the T-shirt with chalk—one center front, one center back, and one on each side just under the bustline. Trim off the bottom of the T-shirt, leaving an inch of seam allowance.

Sewing

Choose your center front decorative panel and pin it onto the center front of the striped T-shirt. If that panel is not long enough, cut two T-shirt parts and sew them to either end of the center panel in order to make a panel about 33" x 63". Pin this panel to the front arch. Pin, then sew a panel to the back of the T-shirt bodice in an arc shape. Cut two more panels from T-shirts to make the two side panels of the skirt. Pin, then sew them to the bodice.

Once the four skirt panels are sewn to the bodice, pin the sides of the panels together and stitch them. Turn the tunic inside out and trim the excess fabric from seams.

Embellishment

Choose some colorful bits from the T-shirt and fabric scraps. Pin them around the neckline to make a pleasing arrangement. Stitch them down and stitch around the neckline three times to include a little decorative stitching. Add a decorative pin.

Tips

• Wacky needlework needs to see the light of day.
• Leggings, anyone?

Grande Fete Tunic

Cowabunga! What more could a girl want in a T-shirt? Sequins, a color wheel full of bright hues, and major graphics make you just want to shoot the moon with this treasure. Find out how much is too much by putting everything you've got into this little Frenchie! Go for it!

Materials

- T-shirt with graphics and embellishments
- 2 T-shirts
- Cup towel
- Fabric remnant
- T-shirt parts
- Vintage button
- Chalk

Preparation

Wash, dry, and press all the components. Draw four arches on the bodice with chalk—one center front, one center back, and one on each side. Trim the excess off the T-shirt leaving about 1" seam allowance.

Cut the cup towel in half to use as the center front skirt panel. This one was about 14" x 16" when cut in half. Cut a skirt side panel (about 13" x 38") from the fabric. Pin these two panels in place. Cut another side panel, about 20" x 14" and a five-sided pentagon-shaped back panel. This piece should measure about 13" x 16" x 15" x 17" x 16".

Sewing

Pin T-shirt sections to the arches on the front, back, and sides of the bodice to form skirt panels. Sew them in place. Next, pin the ends of the side panels together and stitch them. Press and stitch a hem in the woven fabric skirt panel. The knit panels are fine without a hem, or you can place them so that the shirt hem becomes the new tunic hem.

Embellishment

Choose some T-shirt parts and fabric scraps to trim the neckline. Pin, then stitch them in place. To add interest, stitch around the neckline three times. Pin on a vintage message button and you are good to go.

Tips

- Yesterday's T-shirts have a future in your hands.

Call the Marines

Who do we call when we need help? Well, the Marines, of course! Here we call on the Marines to help us work some upcycle magic. Simply simple is this sundress's middle name. Take one T-shirt celebrating our Marines, add one Vera silk scarf, and *voila*! You have an eye-catching little number you could wear anywhere.

Materials

- T-shirt
- Silk scarf—oblong shape 14" x 72"

Preparation

Hand-wash the scarf and T-shirt and carefully press.

Sewing

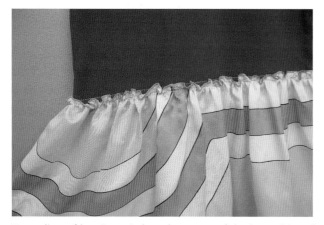

Run a line of basting stitches along one of the long sides of the scarf. Pull the top thread to gather in the scarf so that it fits the bottom edge of the T-shirt. Pin the gathered scarf to the outside of the hem of the T-shirt. Adjust the gathering until it is even all around. Topstitch the scarf to the hem of the T-shirt.

Tips

- Put it on, go somewhere, and be prepared to get compliments!

Pierced Navel Skirt

Why not feature a favorite
concert T-shirt in a new way?
Avoid the same old, same old
by making a fabulous wraparound to feature a too-dear-to-
toss T. All you need are some
worn-out or discarded T-shirts
and a little Wabi-Sabi outlook
on life. This skirt won't be perfect—it won't even be close.
But it is guaranteed to be a
little bit sassy and a little bit
comfy!

Materials

- 8 or 9 T-shirts or parts of T-shirts
- T-shirt with bold graphic
- Pattern for wraparound paneled skirt (optional)
- Newspaper or a paper bag for making patterns

Preparation

Wash, dry, and press your T-shirts so that they are nice and flat to work with. This skirt has five wedge-shaped panels, but they are not all exactly the same size, shape, or length. Lay out your T-shirts and T-shirt parts to design the five panels. Three different purple/lavender shirts made three full-length panels. Cut 1" strips from four different T-shirt scraps. This project used one lavender, two purple, one orange, and one baby blue. (Using the hems of the T-shirts will give you a sturdier waistband.)

Use a purchased pattern or make a pattern for the gore of the skirt using newspaper or a paper bag. Decide the length you want your skirt to be. The skirt will be about five panels around, so the tops of the gores, when sewn together, should be big enough to go around the waist and overlap about 12"–16". Cut out the gores for your skirt.

Sewing

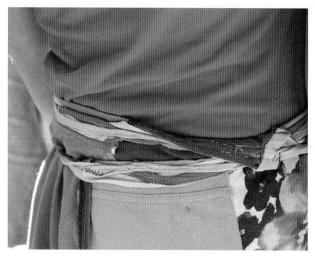

Lay out the panels on a flat surface and fiddle with the arrangement until you are satisfied. Pin together the panels, and then sew them together, overlapping them slightly. Press the seams and try on the skirt to make sure it fits and overlaps appropriately.

To make a simple waistband, use the bottom hems of three T-shirts. Sew down one of the T-shirt bottom pieces starting at one end of the waistband. Next sew down the second band above, below, and over the first band; do the same with the third. Once the waistband is in place, top-stitch in a fanciful way to add a bit of embellishment.

To make the ties for the skirt, cut 1" bands from one or two t-shirts. When the bands are cut, pull them from each end to stretch them out. Sew down one double band at one end of the waist and another at the other end. This will give you a total of four knit streamers, two at each end, to tie your skirt on and to adjust it to fit.

Since the skirt is just one thickness of T-shirt fabric, cut some scraps from a T-shirt or two and sew one down the edge of each end panel. This will add color, reinforce the end panels, and give your skirt a finished look.

Embellishment

Cut out, pin, and sew the bold graphic T-shirt section you have selected to make the big splash on your skirt.

Tips

- Think Wabi Sabi, not perfection or mathematical precision.
- Don't worry if there is a seam in a section of T-shirt you want to use—an existing seam is no problem.

Niner, Niner Skirt

A bunch of old T-shirts and a sewing machine are just about all you will need to make a soft and comfy new four-panel skirt. Niner, Niner might tickle your creative fancy. It is pretty darn easy to make if you are a free-thinking, easygoing, think-outside-the-box kind of a sewer. The colors you choose, the graphics on the fodder shirts you feature, and the way you combine them make each skirt unique. Have some fun, break some rules, and make a fashion statement like no other.

Materials

- Parts of 3 green T-shirts (including 1 with a bold graphic)
- Parts of 4 orange T-shirts (including 3 with bold graphics)
- 1 T-shirt scrap
- Pattern for 4-panel skirt (optional)
- Newspaper or a paper bag for making patterns
- Embroidery thread and needle

Preparation

Wash, dry, and press your T-shirts so that they are nice and flat to work with. Lay out T-shirts and T-shirt parts to design four wedge-shaped panels for the skirt. Parts of three different green and orange shirts together made four full-length panels. Use the pattern or make a wedge-shaped panel pattern from the newspaper or paper bag. The wedge should be 8" across at the top, 12" across the bottom, and 21" long. Use two or three different T-shirt sections to make up some of the panels, paying attention to color placement and light and dark contrasts.

Sewing

Sew the panels together and press seams open. Cut a yoga-style waistband from one of the heavier T-shirts. Cut it about 5" wide and 1" larger than your lower waist-line. Sew the two ends together and press the seams. Pin the waistband to the skirt, right sides together; stitch it in place, then turn it and press. Fold it over and pin the waistband to the inside of the skirt. Hand- or machine-stitch the inside waistband in place.

Embellishment

Use pearl cotton or embroidery thread to sew a cross-stitch pattern up the front seam of the skirt.

Tips

- Think Wabi Sabi, not perfection or mathematical precision.
- If you cut off the hem of a T-shirt, save the part you cut off. Those pieces are perfect for edging the end panels of a skirt or for creating waistbands.
- Add a pocket or two for your cell phone and keys.

Flag Day Top

Love vintage crochet pieces but don't much like to sew? This project is made for you. Start with a T-shirt and three crocheted placemats, add just a tiny bit of sewing, and you have a sassy little number to shake up your wardrobe!

Materials

- Striped T-shirt
- 3 oval crocheted placemats, 20" x 13"
- 3 buttons

Preparation

Put the T-shirt on a dress form. Fold the horizontal top one-third of each of the placemats down over the bottom two-thirds. Pin the top of one folded placemat along the hem of the T-shirt, centering it in the front of the shirt. Pin another folded placemat to the front left side of the shirt and continue pinning it so that it ends at the center back of the T-shirt. Do the same with the final folded placemat on the right side.

Sewing

Sew the placemats to the hem of the T-shirt.

Embellishment

The complicated and exotic crocheted placemats bring almost all the drama you need for this little firecracker. Simply sew a nice vintage red button where each placemat meets the other and save the rest of the embellishments for another day.

Tips

- Honor the handiwork of the women who came before us—use their work in new ways.

CHAPTER 3

Upcycling Sweaters

Sweaters to an upcycler are like crayons to a preschooler. There is no end to the creative possibilities for crayons—or for sweaters. Sweater colors are even more varied than a box of 64, and you can use them no matter what shape they are in. Felt them, shrink them, cut them up, and make sausage out of what is left. Sorry to mix my metaphors but trust me—upcycling old sweaters is more fun and more addictive than binge-watching your favorite TV series. Try it! You'll love it!

White Cashmere and Black Lace

Look like a million dollars while spending less than $10. Elegant, sophisticated, *and* costs less than 10 bucks? No way! Way! The white cashmere sweater rang in at $4, the camisole was $2, and the beautiful wool skirt was on sale for $3 at a local thrift shop. What could be more elegant than white cashmere and black lace? This is not an overly complicated project—it really just alters a sweater and hems a skirt. Sound like fun? Give it a try.

Materials

- White cashmere pullover
- Lacy camisole
- Vintage plaid wool skirt
- Chalk
- Vintage lace—2 types:
  $2^1/2$" wide straight-edge—3 yds.
  1" wide scalloped-edge—$2^1/2$ yds.

Preparation

Begin with a white cashmere pullover. Do not felt the sweater. Draw a chalk line down the center front of the pullover.

Sewing

Zigzag stitch down the front of the sweater on either side of the chalk line. Cut open the front of the sweater between the two stitching lines, making the pullover into a cardigan.

Embellishment

Sweater Center Front

Pin the straight-edge, wider black lace in place down the front middle on each side. Fold under $1/2$" of lace at the hemline. Fold under $1/2$" to the inside center front. Pin the lace in place all the way from the hemline to the neckline. At the neckline, fold under another $1/2$" and pin. Hand-stitch the center edge of the lace in place.

Next, pin the scalloped-edge lace to both sides of the center front. Allow the scalloped-edge lace to very slightly overlap the straight-edge lace. Machine-stitch all the lace in place. Be sure to use black thread on the top and white on the bobbin.

Hemline

Pin the wider lace around the bottom of the sweater just as you did on the center front. Start by tucking $1/2$" of the raw edge under the center front lace trim. Continue around the hemline and finish by tucking in another $1/2$" of raw edge.

Faux Pockets

Cut two strips about $4^1/2$" to 5" long of the $2^1/2$"-wide lace. Press under $1/2$" of the two raw-edge ends of the lace "pockets," choose a spot that suits you on either side of the center front, and pin the "pockets" in place. Once you like the placement, machine-stitch them in place.

Cuffs

Pin the wider lace in place on each cuff, starting at the seam line and turning $1/2$" under the edge of the cuff. Overlap one raw edge of the lace over the other raw edge and tuck under. Hand-stitch in place. Pin in place the top edge of the cuff and hand-stitch. The sleeve will be too small to machine stitch, so hand-sew it.

Neckline

Use the scalloped-edge lace for the neckline. Fold under twice so you don't start with a raw edge. Begin by pinning the lace to the neckline. Tuck under about a $1/2$" every inch or so, making the ruffled effect around the neck. Stitch the lace to the neckline.

Camisole

Find a thrift store cami in lace or lace print to wear under your new Chanel-style cashmere and lace sweater-jacket. Try to find one with an interesting band around the bottom so it can extend below the cardigan.

Skirt

This thrift store find was from the 1960s. It was beautiful wool and beautifully constructed. If you can find a comparable skirt, put it on with the camisole and cardigan and pin up the hem at a nice short length that complements the other components. Cut the skirt off, leaving a 2" hem. Cut the lining off and hem it by turning under $1/4$" and pressing two times. Sew the hem in the lining. Zigzag-stitch the wool skirt along the bottom so that it will have a partially finished edge; pin up the hem, press, and sew in the hem.

Tips

• Large faux pearls and gold or silver chains are de rigueur for the Chanel look.
• Use the hem-stitch mode on your sewing machine to sew the hem in the skirt rather than sewing it by hand.

Green Goddess Sweater

Bet you have a pretty solid-color pullover that you love but are tired of. If not, I bet you there is one just waiting for you at GW*. Rescue and revive a pullover by adding in wedge-shaped side panels to give it swing and roving to make it sing. For next to nothing you can go straight to the front of the stylin' line!

*GW is code for a favorite shop—Goodwill.

Materials

- Upscale, outdated green pullover sweater
- Second sweater in another shade of green
- Wool roving in third shade of green
- Felting needle and brush pad or sponge
- Scrap paper for pattern
- Chalk

Sewing

Start by stitching from the hemline to 2" before the armpit on either side of both side seams of the primary sweater. This will keep the edges from raveling when you cut the seams open. Cut the seams open from the bottom edge to about 2" under the armhole seam.

Make a pattern for the wedge you will cut from the second sweater by laying out the primary sweater so the underarm area of the sweater is visible. Lay the scrap paper under the triangular wedge that was formed when you cut the seam open, and then use the chalk to draw the wedge onto the paper. Once you have drawn your pattern, draw a seam line on the upright sides of the wedge.

Cut out the wedge pattern and lay it out on the second sweater. Place the pattern so that the base of the triangle is on the finished bottom edge of the second sweater. Pin the pattern on the second sweater so that when you cut the wedge out of the second sweater, you will be cutting through both the front and the back of the sweater, giving you two triangles, both with finished edges on the base of the triangular wedges. Zigzag the raw edges of the wedges.

Pin the wedges you have cut from the second sweater into place in the open side seams of the original sweater. Overlap the seams of the first sweater over the wedge to give you a flat seam that will not need to be pressed open.

Start at the bottom finished edge. Make sure the bottom edge of the first sweater side seam is in line with the new wedge bottom edge. Stitch seams and press.

Embellishment

Gild the lily by needle-felting wool roving over the seams where the two sweaters overlap. Lay out the sweater on a solid surface. Lay a short strip of roving over the seam and use the felting needle on top with the felting brush or sponge underneath. Start the process under the arm so that when you get to the hem of the sweater your technique will be perfected.

Tips

- Remove any pilling from the sweaters before you begin.
- If you like the "more is more" look, add more roving to the neckline, or perhaps a running stitch with yarn.

Rule Britannia! Union Jack Sweater

Who can resist the appeal of the graphic design of the flag of Great Britain? That crisp contrast of red and white on a field of deep navy makes such a fashion statement. Everybody has a navy blue sweater or jacket on hand—or at the very least, every thrift store has one. A dig through your notions drawer will surely turn up some rickrack and ribbon remnants. With a little time and some straight stitching, you can rule in your new (old) Rule Britannia sweater.

the jacket. Draw out a flag pattern on the graph paper and make sure it fits in the chalk outline you have drawn on the jacket. Draw the flag's diagonal, vertical, and horizontal lines in chalk on your jacket.

Sewing/Embellishment

The only sewing required on the project is for the embellishment. Measure the length of the two diagonals. Starting with the red bias tape, cut two strips the length of the diagonals plus 2". You are making the trim that you will later sew to the back of the jacket. Stitch the large white rickrack under the edge of the bias tape. (Be sure the bobbin thread is white and the top thread is red so that it won't show.) Next, stitch the white grosgrain ribbon under the other edge of the red bias tape. Cut each of the two diagonal strips in two, crosswise, at the center.

Looking at your flag image, pin in place the four sections of diagonals according to the design plan. Next measure the width and length of the large red cross in the flag. Cut two strips of the red grosgrain. Before attaching it to the coat, stitch the white rickrack under each side of the red crossbar and the vertical bar.

Using navy blue bobbin thread and red top thread, stitch the diagonals in place. Stitch the red tape down on both sides of center and press. Next, using white top thread, stitch the white ribbon in place and press.

Next, again using white top thread, topstitch the horizontal bar of the cross in place and press. Tuck the ends of the strips under about $1/4$" and hand-stitch them in place. Rule Britannia!

Tips

- Use what you have in your stash to interpret the components of the flag.
- What about a French, Italian, or Mexican variation? The map's the limit!

Materials

- Navy blue sweater or boiled wool jacket
- Large ($1/2$") white rickrack—$6^1/2$ yds.
- White $3/8$" grosgrain ribbon—3 to 4 yds.
- Red rayon $3/8$" seam binding—4 yds.
- Red $1^1/2$" grosgrain ribbon—1 yd.
- Image of British flag
- Graph paper and pencil for pattern
- Chalk

Preparations

For this project I used a boiled wool jacket. It was washed in the washer and then dried in the dryer to further felt the wool and shrink the jacket. A pullover or cardigan sweater could be used for this project and work as well.

Felt the boiled wool jacket and try it on to make sure it fits. Find an image of the British flag and decide how long and wide the rectangle shape should be to fit the back of your jacket. Using those measurements, draw a chalk line around the perimeter of that rectangle onto the back of

One-Moth Wonder

One moth + one moth hole = one tossable favorite sweater. Bet you have seen it happen before—one single moth hole in a favorite piece of clothing and it is headed to the landfill. Wait, maybe there is a solution! Cover that moth hole and upcycle that puppy! Covering the moth hole with a magnificent vintage hankie gave this sweater a whole new lease on life. Now it is a little bit sassy, a little bit quirky—in fact, it's a whole different sweater!

Sewing and Embellishment

There is very little sewing on this one—it's only needed to sew the embellishment on. Start by sewing a circle in the center of the hankie. Next sew a ring around the hankie just inside the outer edge. Go back and sew another ring about 1"–2" outside the center circle. Sew the last circle between the third circle and the outer edge ring. Press.

Tips

• Put out a BOLO (Be On the Look Out) to your friends and family for a smashing round hankie. Round ones are scarce!

Materials

• Sweater with moth hole
• Vintage round hankie
• Double-sided iron-on interfacing (size of the hankie)
• Pencil

Preparation

Hand-wash both the sweater and the hankie and press them. Place the hankie on the interfacing and trace around it with a pencil. Cut out the shape you have traced and follow the instructions on the interfacing to iron it onto the hankie. Next place the hankie on the sweater and again follow the instructions to iron the hankie onto the sweater at the spot you have selected.

Orange Juju

A felted wool patchwork tunic in several shade of one color can be a work of art. Orange is such a happy color. Apparently the moths thought so too because they had their way with four perfectly lovely orange sweaters. Oh well, no matter. Just cut them up and make them into an orange work of art.

Materials

- 5 orange sweaters (You might be able to use 4, depending on where the moths have feasted.)
- Yarn and needle
- Bias tape and/or lace hem tape
- Pattern (optional)
- Pin back and scrap of green wool (if you want to make the stringy flower embellishment)

Preparation

Machine-wash the sweaters in hot water to make them felt up. Find a tunic top whose shape you like and use it for your pattern, or choose an actual pattern. I used Simplicity #1614 to get a general shape for the tunic.

Start by designing your eight sections: two top front sections, two top back sections, two lower front sections, and two lower back sections. Fiddle with your fodder sweaters until you arrive at a plan on which sweater will be in which of the eight sections:

- Upper right front—URF
- Upper left front—ULF
- Lower right front—LRF (needs bottom hem)
- Lower left front—LLF (needs bottom hem)
- Upper right back—URB
- Upper left back—ULB
- Lower right back—LRB (needs bottom hem)
- Lower left back—LLB (needs bottom hem)

When you cut out the four lower sections, be sure to place the bottom edge of your pattern on the bottom edge of your felted sweaters. The band along the bottom of the sweaters will become the bottom edge of your tunic, and there will be no need to hem it.

Sewing

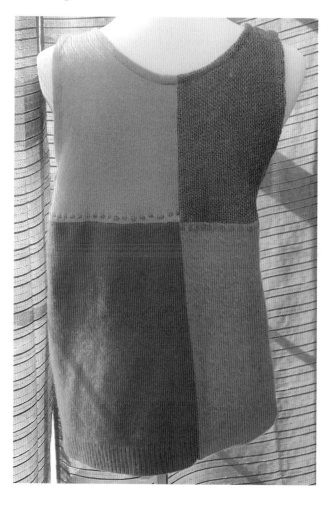

If the wool you have selected for any of your eight sections is not large enough, select a scrap of wool and sew it to the too-small piece to make it fit your pattern piece. I had to do that for both of the top front sections of this one.

Sew the two top front sections together at the center front seam. Sew the two lower front sections together at the center front seam. Repeat the process with the four back sections. Now you have two front sections (uppers and lowers) and two back sections (uppers and lowers).

Pin the two upper top sections together at the shoulders and sew them together. Pin the front lower section to the front upper section and sew them together. Pin, and then sew the upper back sections to the lower back sections, matching the center seam. Pin the sides together and sew the side seams. If your wool is well felted, you will not need to finish the raw edges; but if it is not, serge or zigzag the raw edges of the seams. Sew bias or lace hem tape to the outside edge of the neck and armholes. Turn it under and machine stitch the bias tape down. Press the seams flat.

Embellishment

Sew a running stitch on the front and the back with yarn. Stitch about $3/8"$ above or below the center horizontal front and back seams.

If you want to embellish this even more, gather some slivers of castoff sweaters into a bunch. Sew the bunch together and add a pin back. Pin the felted wool stringy flower to the shoulder of your tunic. Turn to page 16 for a tutorial on making the stringy flower.

Tips

• Wait for someone to say to you, "Orange you beautiful today?!"

Orange Sweater— Homage to Josef Albers

Moths had a feast on the back of this sweater. The sleeves and front were fine, but not the back upper left. Look to art to solve this conundrum with a simple project. German-born American artist Josef Albers was famous for his simple use of color blocking. Why not pay homage to Albers and cover the moth holes at the same time?

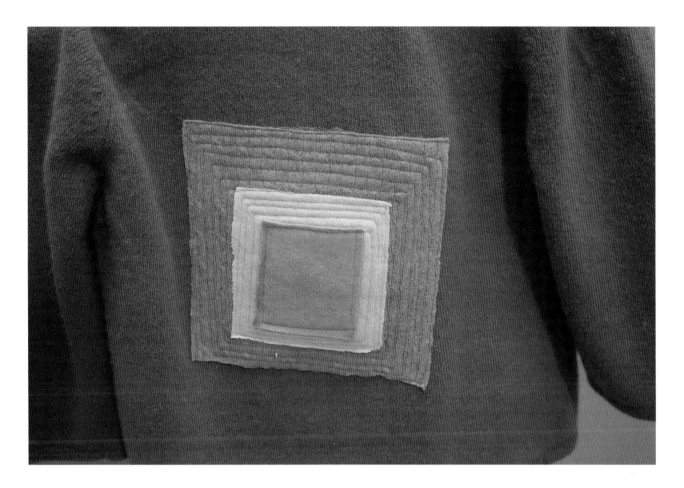

Materials

- Wool sweater
- Scraps of other felted wools in three coordinating colors
- Lightweight iron-on double-sided interfacing (a square for each color patch)
- Rotary cutter and board (optional)
- Pressing cloth

Preparation

Felt the sweater using the method of your choice. This sweater was an extra-large long-sleeved sweater. After felting it, it became a more medium-size sweater with three-quarter-length sleeves. Factor in the possible shrinkage when you choose the sweater you want to recycle. Choose some other sweaters, or other sweater parts, to compose your Josef Albers-inspired color block.

Sewing and Embellishment

The only sewing necessary for this project is the embellishment which conceals the moth damage. Lay out the sweater so that you can "audition" the three colors you have selected for your color blocks.

Once you have selected the three colors, decide in which order you want them to appear. Cut the squares using a rotary cutter and mat if you have them, but regular scissors will work also. Apply the iron-on interfacing to the back side of the three squares. Iron the top square to the second square, then the second square to the third square. Place the third square on the sweater and pin it in place. Press it to the sweater, and then machine-stitch the square patches to the sweater. You can stitch concentric lines in about a $1/4$" pattern, or you can stitch in any pattern you like. The purpose is to make sure the squares are firmly attached to the sweater, covering the moth holes.

Tips

- The square does not need to be centered and does not need to be perfectly upright. Place it where you like it— you're the designer!
- Use a pressing cloth when pressing felted wool. It scorches easily.

Shades of Gray Sweater Dress

Contrast between silky and wooly, stripes and solids, prissy and daring—this project ticks all the boxes for edgy, Mori girl, outside-the-box dressing! Without the silk camisole, the dress is a classic. With the camisole, it's kinky and full of personality. It's your call!

Materials

- Striped wool sweater
- Cable-knit wool sweater
- Silk camisole
- Lace hem tape
- Pattern for cutting the neckline of the top sweater
  (You can use a purchased pattern, or a favorite neckline
  of a top you already own.)
- Silky thread in variegated colors
- Chalk
- Pressing cloth

Preparation

Felt the two sweaters using the method of your choice.
Felting the sweaters will shrink them and slightly distort
their shapes. Just expect this, work around it, and try not
to let it worry you.

Carefully lay a neckline pattern on the striped sweater,
chalk the cutting lines, and cut out the neckline.

Draw a chalk line on the cable-knit sweater from armpit
to armpit. Cut along this line on both the back and front
of the sweater. Turn the sweater upside down so that
the hemline is now the waistband of the skirt. Since the
sweater is felted, it won't need to be hemmed.

Sewing

Lay the bottom edge of the striped sweater slightly over
the new waistband of the sweater that now forms the skirt
of the dress. Pin, and then stitch them together. Using a
press cloth, press the seam line nice and flat.

Pin the lace hem tape to the outside neckline, starting at
the center back. Stitch down the tape 1/4" from the sweater
neckline opening. Turn the seam tape under, and then use
the pressing cloth to press the neckline in place. Pin and
hand-stitch the other edge of the neckline tape in place.

Embellishment

Take the silk camisole and pin four diagonal darts on
either side of the front center line and the back center line,
making a fishbone pattern. Sew the darts in by hand on
the outside of the camisole using colorful variegated silky
embroidery thread. Slip the camisole on over the wooly
dress and go save the world!

Tips

- Add a skinny day-glo orange patent leather belt and
  some spotted knee socks to kick it up a couple of
  notches.
- Always use a press cloth when working with felted
  wool, as it scorches easily.

Patchwork Sweater Dress

What a fun way to utilize scraps of leftover felted wools. The color scheme just "happened" from what was in the felted wool sweater scrap bag. The four sleeves that make up the skirt were left over from other projects. The Wabi Sabi hem on the skirt was just the way the sleeves were left when they were cut out of the sweater bodies used in other designs. The contrast between the tightly matched patchwork of the bodice and the raggedy hemline makes a unique and artsy look. If you are an intermediate or skilled sewer, try this frock on for size.

Preparation

If you don't already have scraps of felted wool, then wash wool sweaters in hot water to felt them. Wash them in color groups because the fuzz transfers from sweater to sweater and will change the colors of the sweaters unless they are washed with like colors. Dry them in a hot dryer with a tennis ball to help them felt.

Fiddle around with the bodice sections of the pattern until you find the sweater scraps that are the right size for each pattern piece. Arrange the pieces on a surface in the form of the bodice front and back to confirm that you like the color placement before you cut out the sections.

Cut out the bodice sections and the interfacing. When cutting out these pieces, be sure to cut the bodice center back seam allowances slightly larger than the pattern; you will need plenty of seam allowance when installing the back zipper. Apply the interfacing to the bodice sections. Cut out the bodice lining, again leaving larger seam allowances on the center back bodice seams.

Materials

- Felted wool sweater scraps for bodice
- 4 sweater sleeves for skirt
- Lightweight, iron-on interfacing
- Lining for bodice
- Pattern of your choice (I used Simplicity 1654D5)
- Heavy metal 16" zipper

Note:
This project is complex and is not for beginners.

Sewing

Follow the directions on the pattern to sew and line the bodice. The pattern directions suggest applying decorative stitching to certain parts of the bodice. I used a simple machine zigzag stitch and black thread, but hand-stitching with lightweight yarn in the color of your choice would also work.

Choose four sweater sleeves and sew them together to form a four-gore skirt. Sew the skirt to the bodice. Sew the zipper to the outside of the center back of the dress.

Embellishment

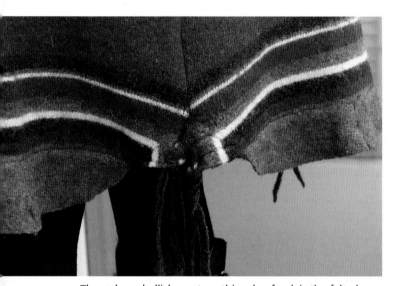

The only embellishment on this edgy frock is the felted wool seams on the bottom of the skirt. Since the bottom of the skirt was sleeves cut from sweaters, they had some scraps of wool seams hanging from them. Rather than cutting them off, enhance them by braiding them and adding a few more. They give a nice Rastafarian look to the hemline. The really big moth holes in the hemline were left as well to keep the dress honest.

Tips

- Use lighter-weight sweaters like cashmere or merino for the bodice. A little heavier sweater will work for the skirt, but don't go too heavy.
- Use lightweight interfacing to keep the bodice from getting too heavy. There are some tricky seams in this project.
- I loved the deconstructed look of the sleeves just as they were cut out of the sweater, but if you prefer a more tailored look, cut the skirt hem off in a clean straight line.
- Upcycle the lining from a worn-out jacket to line the bodice.

CHAPTER 4

Upcycling Menswear

Menswear uses such beautiful, costly fabrics—it would be a crime to put that fabric in the landfill. Men's sweaters tend to come in beautiful muted colors and be knit from pricey imported wools. Take advantage of those fabrics, colors, and tailoring to deconstruct them and make them a little edgy and new again.

Little Black Dress— $5 Wonder

Who would have thunk it? You can make a "silk purse" dress from a "sow's ear" big-box-store men's muscle-man T-shirt. Yes, you can! I snagged this men's sleeveless T-shirt at a big-box store for $4.97—full price. From there I stitched and embellished, added a few bits and bobs, and ended up with a one-of-a-kind LBD. Coco Chanel, eat your heart out!

Materials

- Men's sleeveless muscle-man T-shirt
- Scraps of silky black lining fabric
- Roll of 6"-wide black tulle

Sewing

Try on your big-ole-guy extra-large muscle shirt, wrong-side-out, and taper it by pinning it, starting under the arms and continuing down the side seam at an angle to below the waistline. Stitch these side seams to make the dress pear-shaped. Right-side-out, take two or three box-pleat tucks in the back of the neck and stitch them down at the neckline. Leave the front as a big scooped-neck, but put tucks in the back neck so that the dress will fit you. You will wear a fitted T-shirt or camisole under the creation so don't worry about showing too much skin.

With the shirt right-side-out, make a series of horizontal darts around the bottom of the skirt (which is the bottom of the T-shirt). Make some of the darts at an angle to the bottom of the skirt and some parallel to it. Make the darts about 5" to 6" or less in length and 2" to $2^1/_2$" deep at the deepest point. The purpose of the darts is to shorten the skirt, while at the same time creating texture and movement. If you want to wear it as a shorter tunic, make plenty of length-shortening darts.

Embellishment

Embellish the neckline by making a rose and three wedge-shaped leaves. Find directions for the shaggy lining rose on page 13 and the silky leaves on page 15.

Take a strip of the 6" tulle about a yard long and tie it into a bow. Tack it down over the tucks in the back neckline. Trim the ends to points. Sew tulle to the inside of the hemline, taking tucks in the tulle every few stitches.

Tips

- Keep stitching random horizontal tucks in the skirt until the dress is a length that is pleasing and the tuck pattern looks balanced.
- If you want a more casual look, leave the bottom ruffle of tulle off the dress.
- Consider wearing a skirt or two and some leggings under this for that lagenlook.

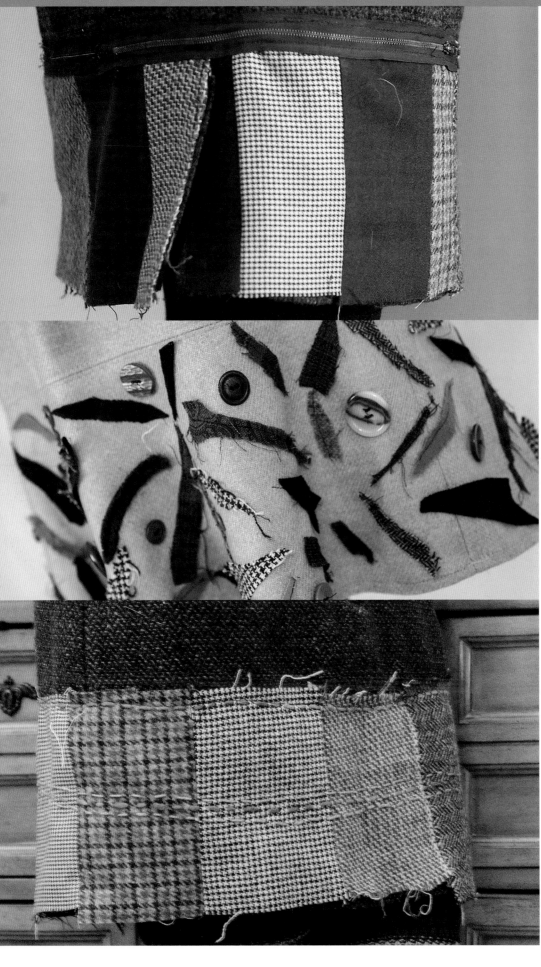

Menswear Kibbles and Bits Trio— Larry, Curly, and Moe

These three little wool skirts were brought back from oblivion with just bits and bobs of woolens and buttons from men's slacks, suits, and sport coats. You can use every little bit of castoff menswear fabric—the colors and weaves are too beautiful to waste. This trio of skirts each started with a ready-made skirt from the archives or the thrift store. Cut up some of hubby's clothes while he is asleep in the recliner to get the necessary scraps of menswear. Just kidding! Choose one of these skirt variations and give it a try!

Skirt 1—Larry

Preparation

Cut pieces of menswear into rectangles that are 6" tall, in widths from about 2½" to 5". This skirt required about fourteen patches to reach all the way around the skirt.

Sewing

Sew the rectangles' short ends together (with a ¼" seam) to make a long string of patches. Lay the string of patches on the lower edge of the skirt so that the raw bottom edge of the band is parallel with the bottom hem of the skirt. Confirm that the strip is long enough to go all the way around the lower section of your skirt. Press under ½" of the top of the strip. Pin it in place about 6" up from the hem of the skirt. Topstitch the band to the skirt all around the skirt. Leave the lower edge of the patchwork strip as raw edges.

Embellishment

Once the patchwork band is sewn to the skirt, it is time to trim it with upcycled zippers. Put your favorite one in front. (This one was ripped out of an old dress and still has fragments of the dress on it!) Add more zippers until you have embellished the seam where the menswear band joins the skirt.

Materials

- Wool skirt
- Scraps of menswear
- Rotary cutter and mat (optional)
- 3 vintage zippers

Tips

- This is a great place to upcycle those old metal zippers.
- Leave the bottom edge raw—it makes the skirt a little edgier!

Skirt 2—Curly

Preparation

Collect a sackful of snippets of wools. Start by choosing one color of wool and pin scraps of it helter-skelter around the flounce of the skirt. Choose a second color and pin bits of it around the flounce. Continue doing this with all the colors in your collection.

Sewing and Embellishment

Sew each strip down to the skirt by stitching right down the center of the strip. (Pretend the strips are leaves and you are sewing in their center veins.) Work your way around the skirt until all the strips are sewn down.

Now add buttons in the spaces between the strips. Two-hole buttons are faster to sew down, but many menswear buttons have four holes.

Tips

- Be brave! You can't go wrong placing your strips and buttons.
- Leave the frays on the raw edges of the scraps—they make the skirt more impressionistic.

Materials

- Drop-waist wool skirt with flounce
- Scraps of wool tweeds and gabardines
- Buttons, 25–30 in assorted colors and shapes

Skirt 3—Moe

Materials

- Wool skirt
- Scraps of menswear
- 2 colors of yarn or string
- Yarn needle

Preparation

Cut pieces of menswear into rectangles that are 6" tall, in widths from about 2 1/2" to 5". This skirt required about eleven patches to reach all the way around the bottom.

Sewing

Sew the short ends of the rectangles together (with a 1/4" seam) to make a long string of patches. Lay the band of patches on the skirt so that the raw bottom edge of the band is parallel with the bottom hem of the skirt. Confirm that the strip is long enough to go all the way around the lower section of your skirt. Pin it in place about 6" up from the hem of the skirt. Topstitch the band around the skirt. Stitch it about 1/4" below the upper raw edge. Leave the lower edge of the patchwork strip as raw edges.

Embellishment

With a yarn needle and yarn, stitch around the entire patchwork band about halfway between the top and bottom of the band. Using a different color of yarn, stitch another line just above your first line, and then another just below the first line. Using the first color of yarn again, stitch over the machine-stitching where you have attached the band to the existing skirt. This should provide some subtle interest to the band.

Tips

- How about some heavy cable-knit tights and a big cozy sweater to top this off?

Three-legged Jumper

Remember how the birds and mice made a frock for Disney's Cinderella out of bits and bobs? That scene inspired me to make this wool jumper out of three legs of men's slacks and a sport coat. Can you imagine using just one leg from three different pairs of wool slacks? Sounds like fun, right? Give this project a try—make something from nothing and be proud of it.

Materials

- Leg from three different pairs of wool slacks
- Men's wool sport coat
- Tailor's chalk
- Bodice pattern or bodice of top that fits you (I loosely used Butterick B5317 for the shape of the top)
- Scraps of wool fabric
- Yarn and needle
- Lining scraps
- Grosgrain ribbon, 2" wide—1$\frac{1}{2}$ yds.
- 3 buttons
- Chalk
- Seam ripper

Preparation

Cut one leg from three different pairs of wool slacks. I used two pairs of wool gabardine and one pair of lightweight wool plaid flannel slacks. Draw a chalk line across the leg just at the crotch seam so that you can harvest the longest possible part of the pant leg. Cut across your chalk line. Open the inseams of the pant legs with a seam ripper and press out all the creases in the fabric.

Lay a bodice pattern on the front of the men's sport coat. You will need to make a center front seam, even if your pattern has no center front seam, in order to capture the two lower front pockets in your bodice. Lay out your pattern so that each of the lower front pocket flaps will be included within the front bodice. Cut the bodice back out of the back of the jacket. Cut 2" bias strips from wool scraps of three different colors. Fold them in half lengthwise and press a fold in them. These will be the trim for the armholes and neckline. Cut out two patch pockets from the wool scraps for the skirt front.

Sewing

Zigzag-stitch all around the edges of the bodice front and back so that the jacket lining is securely fastened to the bodice. The armholes and neckline will be covered with the bias trim later. Sew the front to the back at the shoulders. Press the seams open. Sew the bodice side seams together and press them open.

Sew the three pant legs together upside down so that the bottom, hemmed edge of the slacks forms the top edge of the skirt. Since the pant legs are tapered, the skirt will be fuller at the bottom than at the top. Run two lines of basting stitches starting $\frac{1}{4}$" from the top edge of the skirt. Pull the basting stitches in so that there is fullness in the skirt and it matches the size of the bodice. Pin the skirt to the bodice, easing in the fullness. The skirt edge is "finished" (because it is the hem of the slacks) and is placed over the raw edge of the bodice. Stitch the bodice to the skirt along both lines of basting.

Try the jumper on and mark where you want the hemline. Cut off the excess length. Press under $\frac{1}{2}$", then press under again another $\frac{1}{2}$". Topstitch the hem in place and press.

Embellishment

Pin the wool bias tape that you made to the armholes and the neckline. Pin the tape to the bodice by placing it under the bodice opening. (Once it is stitched down, you will press and trim the seam so that the raw edge of the bias tape comes over to the top of the bodice, and it will be topstitched.) On the armholes, start pinning just behind the center side seam and continue forward from there. Start pinning the neckline bias tape about 3" above the center front. Make sure you use about three different types of wool trim on the neckline. Overlap the new color over the previous color so there is no gap between the different colors of bias tape. Once the tape is pinned down, stitch it to the bodice, clip the seams, and press the tape toward the outside of the bodice. Pin the tape down and topstitch it, making sure you encase the raw edges of the bodice. Press it and sew buttons at the intersections where each color meets the next.

Pin, and then topstitch the 2"-wide grosgrain ribbon down the center front of the jumper. I hand-stitched the ribbon down to make a smoother look. Tie a bow and tack it to the center front of the skirt.

Make the pockets by sewing two different pieces of wool to scrap lining, pressing, and turning them. Pin the pockets to the front panel of the skirt and topstitch to attach them.

Tips

- Don't worry about precision. The three pant legs won't be the same width—just roll with it. Almost nothing about this project is precise.
- This gorgeous orange grosgrain ribbon was an after-Halloween 90 percent off bargain!
- Always remember to make your pockets large enough to hold your cell phone and keys.

Chic Stroller

Spotted on the Champs-Élysées recently were *beaucoup* dark-colored felted or boiled wool patchwork strollers worn with tights, a long scarf, and boots. How to own one without going bankrupt was the challenge. I tried felting and harvesting my own wool from several out-dated men's sweaters. Awaken your inner chic and make your own. *Voila*, your own piece of Paris for *pas de sou*!

Materials

- 6 wool men's sweaters
- Remnant of silky lining fabric
- Tulle
- Scraps of tweed
- Lightweight iron-on interfacing
- Bias tape
- 3 buttons
- Candle, matches, and tweezers
- Chalk

Preparation

First choose your six wool sweaters, making sure they are fairly close in gauge and weight. Choose a method for felting wool sweaters and felt away.

Sewing

Bodice of the Sweater Coat

Use a men's sweater that you have felted to shrink slightly smaller than your size. Measure, mark with chalk, and then cut the sweater entirely open straight down the center front from the neckline through the front hem. Leave the sleeves attached. Try it on and mark a line with pins, then chalk where you want the bodice to end and the skirt of the sweater to begin. Once you have the bodice length, zigzag 1" below the pin line. Cut the lower bodice off, leaving the row of zigzag stitching as the bottom edge of the bodice seam.

Skirt of Sweater Coat

Cut seven sleeves from the other felted sweaters for skirt panels for the new sweater. You will need four different panels (sleeves) for the front and three for the back. Arrange them so that you reserve a large, soft merino sweater sleeve to serve as the center back panel of the coat. It should be slightly fuller than the other panels.

Since the panels are sleeves, they will be slightly gore-shaped. Place the smaller ends (cuffs) up to attach to the bodice and the wider ends to swing as the bottom of the sweater.

Once you have the four front panels and the three back panels carefully cut out of the other sweaters, arrange them, and then sew them together and press open the seams. The center back should be the widest and longest panel. Run two rows of basting stitches along the top of the sewn-together seven-panel skirt and pull the threads until the skirt fits the bodice. Allow a little fullness in the center back. Stitch the skirt to the bodice at the marked chalk line, making sure the center back skirt is centered. Press this seam open and topstitch both sides of the bodice seam.

Facing

Use strips of the other sweaters to make the facing that goes around the opening of the coat. The strips should be cut 3" wide, but the length of each strip will vary, depending on the length of the sweater scraps you have that are 3" wide. Sew these strips together end-to-end in a random pattern until you have one strip long enough to go from the bottom right of the jacket front, all around the neck, and down to the bottom left. Press seams open. Cut a 3"-wide strip of lining for the back side of the facing. Sew the lining strip to the wool strip with a $1/4$" seam allowance and press open. Cut a strip of interfacing $2^1/2$" wide and as long as the facing. Press the interfacing to the wrong side of the wool facing. Start at one end of the facing and topstitch together the facing and the lining. Stitch in undulating curves down the wool side of the facing. Leave a $1/2$"-wide edge unstitched where you will sew the facing to the sweater. Turn around at the end and stitch back the other way in the same gently curving manner. Continue to do this until the wool and lining are stitched together in a decorative trapunto pattern.

Pin, then stitch the open wool edge to the sweater, allowing plenty of extra facing on each end. Try the sweater on and pin the bottom to create a gently sloping hemline from front to back. Tuck in the raw edges of the ends of the facing and stitch them into place. Pin, stitch, and press bias hem tape to the right-side hemline. Turn it under, press, and hand-stitch the hem tape to the jacket.

Embellishment

Make three wooly amoeba roses and sew them to the center back section of the sweater where the skirt and bodice meet. See page 18 for directions on making the wooly amoeba roses.

Tips

- Use the Internet to find techniques for felting wool.
- Make a large rose with a pin back if you want a closing for the front.
- Don't try to pair a heavy ski sweater with a lightweight cashmere one. They won't play well together in this project.

CHAPTER 5

Upcycling Suits, Coats, and Jackets

A lonesome pink silk or linen jacket at the thrift shop could heat up a tired wardrobe. There are legions of jackets and coats hanging in closets and thrift shops just waiting for a new lease on life. You could be their Pygmalion and convert them into delectable runway winners. Anybody can sew down strips of ribbon or poke some roving into a wool coat. You won't know what you can do until you give it a try!

Jackie Oh! Times Three

Coco Chanel, eat your heart out! Any girl can have a lovely, photogenic, pink Chanel-style fashion—all she needs is a discarded pink jacket and some bits and bobs of trim. A little faux pocket here, a little lace collar there—just add multiple strands of pearls and a pair of sunglasses, and she is ready to meet the press!

Jackie Oh! Jacket 1

This is a simple but effective transition technique for any jacket. It is an easy upcycle that needs only the four faux front pockets and a bow sash in the back to transform this jacket from blah to brilliant!

Materials

- Hot pink jacket with nubby, tweedy, Chanel-like texture
- Black grosgrain ribbon, 1/4" wide—3 1/2 yds.
- Black satin wired ribbon, 2" wide—1 yd.
- Safety pin or pin back

Embellishment

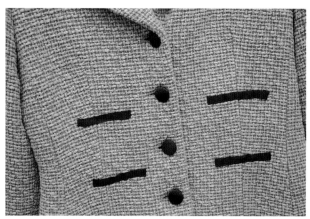

Cut four strips of grosgrain ribbon 3" long and press under 1/2" on each end. Zigzag-stitch the 1/4" hem on all four ends. These will become your four faux pockets. Pin them in place on either side of the front jacket opening, placing two on each side. Try on the jacket and confirm that you are satisfied with the placement. Sew the ribbon strips in place by hand, being careful to attach them only to the jacket fabric and not the lining. Cut a wire-edged ribbon about 1 yard long. Tie the back sash into a sassy bow and cut the ends in points. Sew a pin back to the bow and pin it on the back of the jacket at the waistline.

Tips

- If the buttons on your jacket are not black, cut them off and substitute black buttons.

Jackie Oh, Oh! Jacket 2

Start with a short jacket that follows the waistline. This one is lovely pale lightweight linen that is not lined. It is perfect for summer.

Materials

- Pale pink linen jacket
- Black satin ribbon, 3/4" wide—2 1/2 yds. (or enough to go around the outside of the collar and circle the cuffs)
- Black grosgrain ribbon, 1/4" wide—1/2 yd.

Embellishment

Use the black satin ribbon in place of the traditional Chanel-style braid. It is easier to work with than braid and is lightweight like the jacket. Pin the black ribbon to the outside of the jacket collar. Start by pinning under about 1/2" in a pattern following the angle the collar takes where it attaches to the jacket. Pin down the ribbon all around the jacket and end by tucking under another 1/2". Sew the black ribbon down to the collar, stitching on both edges of the ribbon so that it lays flat on the collar.

Cut four 3" strips of black grosgrain ribbon that will be the faux pockets on the jacket front. Press under 1/2" on each of the four ends. Pin the four strips of ribbon to the front of the jacket where they look the best on you. If your jacket is unlined like this one, you can use the sewing machine to sew these on. If it is lined, you will need to hand-stitch them in place, being careful not to stitch through the lining.

Pin the satin ribbon to the sleeve where the cuff and the sleeve meet. Tuck under the end of the ribbon as you complete the circle. Stitch the ribbon down. Tie two bows with the black satin ribbon and tack them down at the center of the sleeve band. Cut the ends of the ribbons on the diagonal.

Tips

- You can't go wrong with a signature Chanel camellia (see page 8) pinned to the collar, but a scrap dragon flower also looks sensational. See page 12 for directions for this scrap dragon.

Jackie Oh, Oh, Oh! Jacket 3

This project started with a $4 pink genuine silk quilted suit with a nasty stain on the skirt front. In order to be wearable, the jacket needed to be updated from the '90s, but the lovely fabric was worth upcycling.

Materials

- Quilted pink jacket
- Black lace—$1/2$ yd., or enough to cover the collar
- Black braid trim—enough to go around the outside edge of the collar and to make four faux pockets
- Needle and thread
- Fray Check or similar anti-fray product

Embellishment

Lay the jacket out on your cutting table and overlay the collar with black lace. This piece was a small remnant that worked perfectly—it was just enough to cover the collar. Pin the lace to the collar and leave a 1" to $1^1/2$" seam allowance. Keep adjusting the lace pins until you are certain you have completely covered the entire collar, including the part that rolls under the neckline to the jacket lining. Make sure you have plenty of tuck-in seam allowance all around. Allow at least a 1" margin. When you are certain you have done that, carefully cut out the lace collar while it is pinned to the jacket.

Now tuck in the seam allowance under the outside edge of the collar and then the inside edge. Very carefully pin those in place. Using needle and thread, sew the lace down all around the collar, hiding your stitches. Next, place the braid trim on the outside edge of the collar. Pin it down carefully all around the collar, leaving about 1" extra on either end. Hand-stitch the braid in place all around the collar, giving extra care to the beginning and ending sections. Fiddle with them until they look just right. Daub them with a little product to prevent fraying and let it dry, just for security.

Cut four 3" sections of braid trim. Turn under $1/2$" on each end and press. Zigzag-stitch all four ends so they will not fray. Pin two of these faux "pockets" just above the waistline and two just below. Try on the jacket and adjust the pocket placement to where they look the best on you. When you are pleased with the placement, hand-stitch the faux pockets in place.

Tips

- A stretchy black lace shell works beautifully with any one of these three Chanel-style jackets.
- Pearls are a must!

Le Smoking Jacket

This project is a new twist on the iconic Yves St. Laurent 1970s well-tailored velvet jacket famously called *Le Smoking*. It is still in fashion, but no longer on the cutting edge—and certainly not for smoking. Letting your heart and hands loose on a tailored velvet jacket will feel good and pay off. This one went from *Le Smoking* to *Le Smoking Hot*. It's all about the icing on this cake! Roll up your sleeves, grab your scrap bags, and let your inner creativity rip!

Materials

- Velvet blazer
- Scrap of floral fabric
- Green leaf trim—1 yd.
- Scraps of menswear wool flannel and gabardine
- Tulle—6"-wide roll of brown; scraps of red, brown, and green
- Yarn and needle
- 30 buttons for front edge trim
- 34 small buttons in red and pink
- Fabric glue
- 3 zippers (vintage metal are nicest)
- Buckle
- Seam cut from wool jacket

Preparation

Start with a tailored velvet jacket in a color you like. Gather scraps, zippers, and buttons in shades that complement the jacket.

Embellishment

Jacket Front

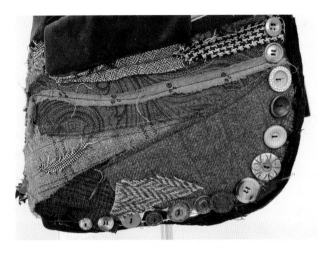

Put the jacket on a dress form or hanger and begin pinning your scraps on the jacket. The plan is to cover over the lower right front of the jacket with some muted colors and a variety of textures. Start at the right front, just under the pocket flap, and pin fabric scraps, repositioning them until you have a pleasing design. Pin on the larger underlayer pieces and sew them down first. Next add some other colors and textures to your target zone. Once your fabric strips and scraps are sewn in place, add a piece of wool along the lower right edge of the jacket, from the second button on down, around the lower front edge, and onto the back of the jacket. I cut this piece from a wool blazer— it was just a curved seam from an old jacket. It provided an edge finish and added structure.

On the lower left front of the jacket pin down three zippers in varying colors and lengths. Topstitch them in place. Make sure one of them is long enough to wrap around to the lower back left of the jacket. Sew a small buckle from the bottom left pocket flap to the lower pocket. This one was from an old plaid kilt.

Cut out a rose and rosebud pattern from a vintage piece of clothing or a remnant. Place it on the right shoulder of the jacket and pin in place. When you are pleased with the placement, hand-stitch it in place. Take buttons in the colors of the rose and sew them on the rose pattern to add texture. I used thirty-four pink and red buttons. The rose appliqué should extend down the front of the jacket and trail over the shoulder and down the back a little. Cut scraps of tulle in the colors of the roses and leaves into tiny, whimsical shapes; cut some green and brown tulle into leaf shapes. Using the heat from a candle, melt the edges of the whimsies and leaves. See page 17 for directions.

Once you have produced the tulle leaves and whimsies, tuck them into the rose shoulder design and pin them in place. Put two or three tiny dots of fabric glue down on the leaf design and glue each tulle leaf in place. Do the same with the rose-colored tulle whimsies, placing them in between the buttons you have already sewn on. The objective of this process is to mute the effect of the rose appliqué and give it a more "smoky" look.

Choose some vintage buttons in colors that complement the jacket's color scheme. This jacket has three actual working buttons on the front. I sewed two buttons between the first two buttonholes on the front. Then I added more buttons, bumper-to-bumper, down the front of the jacket and all the way around past the side seam on both the sides, for a total of about thirty buttons.

Jacket Back

Where the leaves of the rose appliqué extend down a little onto the jacket back, add the small silky leaf trim in three paths. Pin, then hand-stitch them in place.

Jacket Sleeves

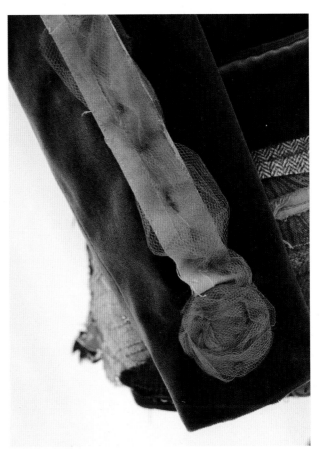

Cut a long scrap of fabric—this one was from a vintage pair of slacks—and pin it in place vertically on the center of the right jacket sleeve. Using a 6"-wide roll of brown tulle, form a small tulle rose at the top of the sleeve, and pin it in place on top of the fabric scrap. Continue with the tulle and pin it down about 3" below the rose. Continue pinning the tulle to the sleeve about every 3" down the sleeve. End by forming and pinning a rose at the end of the sleeve. Select a yarn in a coordinating color, thread a yarn needle, and stitch in place the tulle rose, the fabric scrap, and the tulle. Tack down the tulle at each spot where you have pinned it. Stitch all the way down the sleeve with the yarn, keeping one hand inside the sleeve so you don't sew the arm shut.

Tips

• Don't overthink this project. Just use the notions to "paint" interest onto the blank canvas of the jacket.

Wool Coat

This beautiful 1990s wool coat was in perfect shape, but the style was just a little yesterday blah. It needed color and an update to the 21st century. Seeing a smashing coat dress on the Dolce & Gabbana runway that had some vividly colored stylized flowers gave me inspiration for the perfect solution: I could make similar flowers by felting them. If you have not tried felting wool roving with needles, you have missed some fun. For very little cost and not much energy exertion you could learn a new skill and add life to a tired wool coat. This process should work for any wool coat, jacket, or sweater. This project has almost no sewing involved. Find an unlined wool coat. This one was totally reversible— brown on one side and loden green on the other. This coat was maxi-length but wanted to be a shorter jacket. (If you left it the length it was you would have a no-sew project.) It is still pretty on both sides. Enjoy!

Materials

- Wool coat without lining (this one is reversible)
- Wool felting needles and felting brush or sponge
- Scraps of colored felt or 8½" x 11" sheets of lightweight craft store felt
- Wool roving in colors of your design (6 colors)

Preparation

Choose the colors you want for the flowers on your coat and purchase the wool roving. You can find it in some yarn shops and many places online. Sketch some free-form flowers.

Sewing

The only sewing involved in this project is to serge the lower edge if you shorten it from a coat to a jacket. (If you don't have a serger, find someone who has one and see if you can trade her something for serging the bottom of your new jacket.) Measure carefully where you want the bottom of the jacket to be and chalk a line to cut along. Cut and serge the new bottom edge.

Embellishment

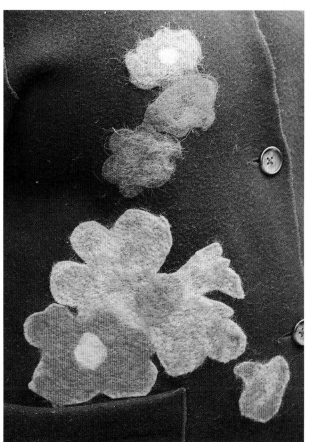

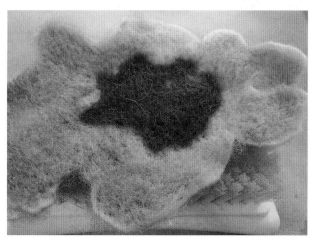

This project is all about the embellishment. Learn to make these felted flowers on page 9.

Gather the felt scraps and wool roving in the colors you want. Draw your "flower" designs on recycled card stock (from your piles of junk mail). Cut out the card-stock flowers and pin them to your coat. Is the scale right? If not, resize your designs and repin them until you are pleased with the overall design.

To make a flower, place a pattern on a piece of lightweight felt and draw around it. Cut the shape out of the piece of felt and place it on the felting brush or sponge. Pull a 1" to 2" hank of roving, spread it apart, and place it on the felt flower. Put on one layer of roving going horizontally on the flower, and then another layer going vertically. Make sure your flower is placed carefully on the felting brush or sponge, and use the felting needle to start punching. Carefully punch away, checking every now and then to make sure the roving is adhering properly to the felt.

Once all the flowers are felted to the lightweight felt, place them on the coat and pin them in place. Felt each of the flowers directly to the coat. Adjust the coat on the felting brush so that all the parts of the flower can be felted to the coat. The "wrong" side of the coat will be beautiful too. It will look like an Impressionist painting.

Tips

- Start with an unlined wool jacket or coat. Shop the thrifts until you find one.
- Another way to make felt flowers is to Nuno felt them. See Internet tutorials for Nuno felting instructions.
- Buy the cheap sheets of lightweight felt in the craft department.
- If you are really brave, felt the roving directly onto the coat without first adhering it to the felt sheets.

CHAPTER 6

Upcycling Scraps and Stash

Something from nothing is a concept most people love. Making wearable clothing from the scrap bag, ripped-up old clothing and linens, little pieces of fabrics brought home from exotic places, and bundles of decorator sample swatches feels pretty darn resourceful and satisfying. Not to mention way fashionable! This could be your new favorite way to save the earth!

Hodgepodge Pink and Blue Tunic

Casual and perky, charming and quirky! What more could you ask of some obsolete blouses and blouse parts? Make this your own project by incorporating some of your favorite blast-from-the-past shirts. Sport the deconstructed look with these raw edges and be fashion forward for next to nothing.

Materials

- Blue-and-white checked linen blouse
- Scraps of fabric
- Assorted parts (especially sleeves) from other cotton and linen blouses
- 2 zippers
- Scraps of crochet
- Pattern (optional)
- Seam ripper

Preparation

Cut the sleeves out of the blouse, sew the front shut, and cut off the buttons. Lay bodice pattern on the shirt and cut the top of the shirt along the lines of the top of the pattern bodice. Cut out a yoke for the tunic from a sleeve of a discarded blouse. I used Simplicity 1466AA to cut the top of the bodice and the yoke for the neckline.

Cut or rip scraps into strips 1" to 3" wide and in a variety of lengths. Dampen and iron the strips.

Using a seam ripper, remove the pocket from the base blouse. Set it aside for reuse on the new tunic.

Sewing

Start at the hemline at the lower back and begin sewing the fabric strips down horizontally around the tunic. Add another strip as one is sewn down. You are covering the shirt like a mummy with one strip of fabric after another. Sew the strips down, capturing each strip and sewing it to the base shirt.

Embellishment

Sew one zipper somewhere on the front of the tunic and one on the back. Add a strip or two of crochet edging over the fabric strips. Tack a small crocheted flower on the yoke of the tunic. Sew the pocket from the original shirt on the right front of the new tunic, put your phone in the pocket, and head out for some fun!

Tips

- If you prefer a level hemline rather than the shirttail showing beneath the tunic, tuck it under and hem it.
- If you prefer a finished edge on the armholes, stitch bias tape around them, turn them under, and stitch them in place.
- Be sure to leave a few areas of the underlying blouse showing—don't cover it all with the strips.

Ombre Scarf

Have you seen these scarves in museum gift shops and longed for one of your own but didn't want to spend *beaucoup* bucks for it? Make one yourself with not much more than a bunch of bite-size scraps! This is not an easy project, but it is certainly a satisfying one. The initial investment for the water soluble product that is the basis for the scarf is pricey, but not nearly as pricey as a ready-made scarf. Satisfy your inner saver and make a beautiful scarf out of nothing but scraps.

space for a while, so don't start work at the kitchen table just before dinnertime. Line up your sandwich bags of colors on the table along the length of what will be the scarf.

Black goes on one end, and the lightest color of robin's egg blue goes on the other end. Start by sprinkling bits of black scraps heavily at the black end, and then gradually sprinkle fewer, with more space between them, as you aim for the center mark of the scarf. Starting at the other end of the scarf, sprinkle the lightest color of blue heavily, and then taper off with just a very few scraps past the middle point.

Follow this procedure, sprinkling charcoal scraps in the next section past the black; let a few charcoals land in the black area. Next sprinkle the dark brown scraps, with a few in the charcoal area and more toward the middle. The lighter brown and rust scraps should be the predominant colors in the center area and continue more lightly out to the blue end.

Now move down to the blue end and lay out the other shades of blue following the same pattern of going more lightly as you head toward the middle. Use the lighter gray shades as you meet up with the rust and brown areas. Your scarf should be almost filled in by now. Don't sneeze on it!

Materials

- Strip of 18" x 72" water-soluble stabilizer (I used Sulky Ultra Solvy)
- Scraps of ribbon, string, thread, lace hem tape, rayon hem tape, lace, fabric selvedges, silk, velvet, and wool
- Sandwich bags
- Iron

Preparation

This project requires a fun preparation time. It is best to start early collecting ribbons, strings, hem tape, lace hem tape, selvedges, bits of wool, velvet, and silk. The more variety you have in your ombre scarf, the more beautiful and unique it will be. Be patient and collect a lot of bits in the colors you want to include. The colors I included in this scarf were robin's egg blue, blue-green, gray-blue, gray, rust, brown, charcoal, and black. I used sandwich bags to store the different colors.

Each tiny piece that you will include in the scarf needs to be cut or torn. I cut them on the diagonal in lengths from 1" to 3". I tear seam tape down the middle to make two skinnier, hairier strips. I also cut strips of lace hem tape and other lace down the middle so that the strips are slimmer.

Cut a strip of water-soluble product about 72" long and lay it out. I used Ultra Solvy Water Soluble Stabilizer by Sulky. It will be a double-wide folded strip, so open it up like you would open a piano bench. Lay the "lid" back so that you can concentrate your effort on the side that would be the piano bench.

The ironing board or a big long tabletop is a good place to start your project. You will need to work at the

Look at the scarf and decide whether the scraps are evenly distributed and the ombre color effect is the way you want it. Rearrange or add more scraps to make it just the way you like it. When it is just right, carefully shut the lid—meaning bring the folded-back sticky side of the product down onto the scarf.

Follow the manufacturer's directions for activating the sticking agent in the stabilizer.

Sewing

Let the sewing begin! Start sewing at the blue end of the scarf and stitch straight down the right side of the length of the scarf to the very end. Turn the corner and stitch down about 1" and turn the corner again, heading back toward the blue end. Stitch the entire length of the scarf from the black end to the blue end in a line parallel to the first line of stitching. When you get back to the blue end, stitch back up to the corner where you started, then back down to about an inch below the second line of stitching. Stitch a third row, turn the corner, and repeat. I stitched fourteen long horizontal rows in this manner.

Next, sew the short vertical rows across the scarf in the same way. Start at the blue end and sew straight down the blue end, over an inch, then back up to the top of that row. Repeat until you get to the other end of the scarf. I sewed more than two hundred of the short rows. Sew all the way around the outer edges of the rectangle two times to make a sturdy outer edge for the scarf.

When all the stitching is complete, follow the manufacturer's directions for dissolving the stabilizer and drying the scarf.

Embellishment

The sewing of this scarf is really part of the embellishment. No more is needed.

Tips

- Let your imagination run free as you consider color combinations for your scarf.
- Start collecting ribbons and scraps now so you will have a broad variety of colors and textures.
- If your sewing machine has a "needle down" position, use it as you sew these rows.
- Your bobbin threads show too, so choose that thread carefully.

Lavender's Blue

The smell of French lavender and the melody of the simple song about Lavender's Blue are enough to make a soft spot in your heart for the color lavender. If you love lavender, watch for the color when you are in thrift stores, searching remnant bins, and when cleaning out your closet.

Note:

This project is not for beginners or for extremely left-brain, logical, sequential thinkers. It is complex, requires flexibility, and will be an adventure.

Materials

- Scraps of blue and lavender fabrics, including laces
- Silky blue camisole
- Purple velvet camisole
- Sleeveless T-shirt or knit pajama top
- Assorted silk flowers
- Tulle—lavender, pale blue, and violet
- Ribbons—lavender and blue scraps
- Remnant of organza—$1/2$ yd.
- Elastic for skirt waistband
- Seam ripper

Preparation

Start collecting recyclable clothing and fabrics in a color group that you prefer. This skirt has bits and pieces from worn-out or stained linen slacks, silk blouses, linen blouses—you name it. Anything is fair game if it is no longer worn. Remnants can make a huge difference when doing projects like this—the 1/3 of a yard of lace I found just made this skirt. Plan ahead for this kind of project and be sure and ask friends and family for castoffs in your color group.

Once you have an adequate stash of fabric, start by ripping strips for the skirt. Straight strips work, but you will need wedge-shaped strips as well. The strips on this skirt range in depth from about 2" to about $6^1/2$". The strips should vary in length because you are harvesting them from different sources. Be sure to include some sheer fabrics. Pleating the strips will make them even shorter, so keep that in mind as you harvest strips. This skirt used about thirty-five strips, but make more than that so that you have options for placement. I like to vary rows with light and dark, sheer and woven, long and short.

Pleating the strips for the skirt is a project by itself. Begin by pressing all your strips. Spritz the fabric with water, and then press the pleat into the strip. Continue to press in the pleats until you have pleated each strip. On some strips make the pleats close together, and on others leave more space between the pleats. Next, take the strips to the sewing machine and sew along the top edge of each strip about $1/4$" from the edge. Use a pointed poker like a seam ripper to make the pleats behave by poking them under the presser foot as you go. Once you have all your strips pleated, add a bit of tulle to some of them. I like to add tulle to some of the lace strips and some of the organza ones. To attach the tulle, lay it over an already pleated strip and use the seam ripper to poke pleats into the tulle as you stitch. I added tulle to about eight or nine of the strips that I used for this skirt.

Sewing

Top

Use a silky camisole for the top of this project. Keep it simple since the skirt will be heavily embellished. Lay out the camisole facedown. Find a blue ribbon about 36" long. Cut it in half, then fold under all four ends about $1/2$" to $3/4$" and press. Pin each ribbon to the camisole back in gentle "C" curves to either side of the back. Use 1"-wide castoff packing ribbon and cut eight 3" sections. Fold each section in half, then fold the raw ends double and pin all eight of them. Sew the raw ends of each section together with a $1/4$" seam allowance. Pin four of these loops under the left ribbon and four under the right ribbon, all facing toward the center back. Once the two long ribbons are sewn in place, the loops will serve as carriers for the long ribbon, which will lace the camisole into a corset shape to give it a better fit. You will also need ribbon to use to lace up the corset. It should be at least an inch wide and at least a yard long.

Lower Skirt

Cut a lower skirt from the T-shirt or pajama top by drawing a horizontal line from armpit to armpit. Cut across this line, leaving an A-line–shaped lower skirt. This will form the base of the lower section of the skirt. Make sure it fits around your hips with a little room to spare. Using remnants, cut out two elongated triangular wedges about $4^1/_2$" or 5" wide by 18" long. Sew one of the sections to the bottom front left of the skirt and one to the lower back right edge of the skirt. These will give the skirt an uneven hemline in front and back.

Upper Skirt

The upper skirt forms the torso section of the skirt. Choose a remnant and wrap it around you so that you can pin a seam, making it fit loosely around your torso. Make sure the lower edge of this piece fits properly to the top edge of the lower skirt (which you made in the previous section). Cut a short upper-skirt section, about 12", from the remnant of silky blue fabric, leaving a seam allowance for one seam. Cut the top of the skirt about 3" taller than you need so you can fold it down to form a waistband casing for elastic. Sew the seam for the upper section. Fold over $1/4$" of the top waist and press. Fold down another generous inch, press, and pin. Sew the casing down, leaving an opening in the back to use for inserting the elastic later. Pin, then sew the upper skirt to the lower skirt.

Embellishing
Upper Skirt

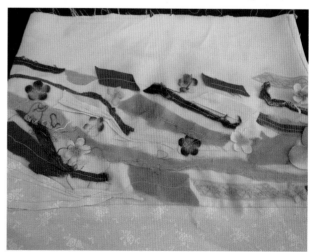

Using scraps of ribbon, stitch ribbons in a horizontal, free-motion, intermittent pattern around the torso section of the skirt.

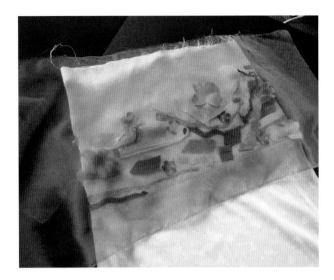

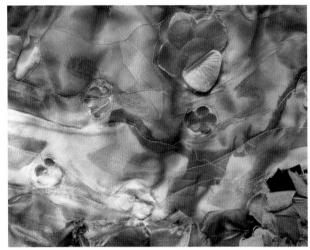

Lower Skirt

Take existing silk flowers apart and use only the parts that please you. Place the flower parts around the upper skirt in a random pattern. Use the sewing machine to tack them down. Cut a piece of organza fabric in a darker color than the upper-skirt base fabric. Cut it the same size as the upper skirt, leaving a seam allowance at the bottom and the 3" allowance at the top to fold over the waistband.

Topstitch around the top skirt section about five times, sewing the organza down in a slightly wavy pattern. Next, stitch a circle around each of the flowers that are now covered by the organza. Once the circles are sewn around the flowers, tack down the center of each flower with an in-place zigzag stitch. Use sharp pointed scissors and cut about 1/8" inside the stitched circle. This will loosen the outside edges of the organza and give the flowers a more dimensional look.

Rip some organza into strips about 2" wide. You will need enough length to go around your hip line about 1 1/2 times. Melt all the edges of the strips so that they curl a little. Pin the strips end-to-end, covering the seam between the upper and lower skirt sections. Pin the end, allowing some slack, and place another pin about 2" from the first. Repeat this around the skirt, covering the seam. This forms a bunting-like band or festoon around the skirt and covers both the tops of the pleated bands of the lower skirt and the topstitched base of the upper skirt. Tack down the festoon and remove the pins. Run the elastic through the waistband and sew the ends together.

Tulle Tufts

Make six tulle tufts—two from each color of tulle. Cut the pieces about 6" square. Using a candle, melt the edges of the tulle, and then melt several holes throughout the body of the tulle strips. Singe the edges of the squares using the candle and tweezers method. Once the edges are singed, pinch the center of the square and tack the pinch on the sewing machine. Tuck the tulle tufts in spots between the pleated bands in the skirt. "Plant" three in front and three in back. See page 17 for directions for making tulle tufts.

Tips

• If you want your skirt to be shaded in an ombre effect, start by sewing the dark strips at the bottom of the skirt, and then use progressively lighter-colored strips as you move toward the top of the skirt.

Silky Stripper

Lovely silk blouses that have gone out of style can have a second chance at a productive life. Rip them into strips, sew them to a silk base blouse, and *voila*! You have a charming, one-of-a-kind silk tunic that is bound to turn heads.

Materials

- 7 or 8 different silk blouses to rip for strips
- Silk blouse for the base—find a blouse with a small keyhole neck opening in the back
- Package of rayon seam tape

Preparation

Choose one of the blouses to serve as the base for the new blouse. Cut the sleeves out of the base blouse, leaving about 1" of the sleeve around the armholes. Hand-wash and air-dry the silk blouses. Cut 2" slits in the other blouses, and then rip several 2" strips from them. Repeat until you have *beaucoup* 2" strips—enough to cover the back and front of the tunic, overlapping slightly.

Sewing

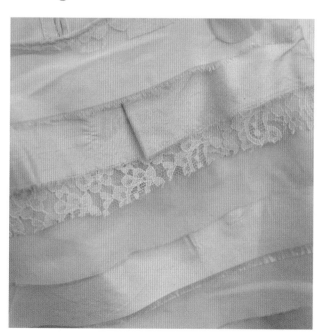

Start just above the hemline at the back of the base blouse. Place the strip horizontally so that it extends below the base blouse hemline about an inch. Stitch down the first strip about $1/4$" from its top edge. When that strip is sewn down, pick up another strip of a different texture and sew it down. Continue the process as though you were stitching down mummy strips from the hem of the base blouse all the way to the top. Each new strip overlaps the one below just slightly so the stitching from the row below doesn't show.

Finish the armholes and neckline by machine-stitching bias tape to the outside. Press the tape, turn it under, trim the excess, and hand-stitch it to the inside of the tunic.

Embellishment

This blouse/tunic can go without embellishment because of its rich texture. If you must embellish it, how about a Chanel-inspired camellia? See page 8 for instructions and required supplies for making this lovely flower.

Tips

- A strand of pearls and some silk pants or a skirt will make an outfit for an evening out.
- Choose a base blouse that has a small back keyhole neck opening with a button to make this project easy.

Tribal Tunic

Beautiful hand-printed fabrics from exotic places are plentiful at estate sales. Someone traveled afar, admired the beautiful textiles, brought some home, packed them away, and forgot about them. It is almost our duty to make something useful from long-forgotten works of art. They are often a one-of-a-kind print and deserve the honor of being worn.

Materials

- Strip of hand-printed fabric, 1½ yds. by 31"
- Lace or rayon bias hem tape
- 18 to 20 assorted buttons
- Top to use as pattern (sleeveless and collarless works best)
- Chalk and yardstick

Preparation

Hand-wash the fabric in cold water and let it air-dry. Fold the cloth in half horizontally. Lay the top you are using for the pattern on top of the fabric. Chalk around the neckline and armholes of the top, leaving a chalk line for your cutting line. Leave a ⅝" seam allowance. Using a yardstick, draw a chalk line from the armhole to the bottom selvage of the fabric on the right and left sides of the top for the cutting lines. Cut out the top front. Flip the fabric over and place the back of the pattern top on the fabric. Mark the outline with chalk. Chalk the side seams using the new front of the top as a guide.

Sewing

With right sides together, sew the shoulder and side seams together and press them open. Press under ¼" along the bottom edge of the new top. Fold it under once more, press, and stitch a shirttail hem.

Stitch the bias tape to the right side of the bodice neck and armholes. Press it under, trim it, pin it in place, and stitch the neck and armholes.

Embellishment

Select an assortment of buttons in variations of the colors of your fabric. Sew the largest button to the center front neckline. Arrange the buttons in a pleasing design around the front neckline of the tunic and sew them in place.

From scraps cut out a cell-phone pocket for your tunic. This one started as a horseshoe shape about 8" by 7". Fold under and press a 1" hem in the top of the pocket. Fold under and press about ½" on three sides of the pocket. Pin, then stitch the pocket in place at the spot that looks the best.

Tips

- Artisan-dyed fabrics might not be colorfast. Hand-wash first to make sure that it is worth your time to upcycle.

Fortuny-style Cloak

Spanish-born designer Mario Fortuny lived and designed gorgeous fabrics in Venice, Italy. He was famous for his luscious patterned fabrics and pleated silk. I found a bundle of patterned fabric samples for sale in an antique mall for $12. They weren't Fortuny, but they certainly paid homage to his style. Although not one sample matched another, the colors and patterns of the different swatches were striking together. What to make of them? Well, an Art Nouveau opera cloak, of course! What could you wear that would make a bigger, more beautiful entrance, for Pete's sake?!

Materials

- Decorator fabric samples (at least 20 13" x 17" swatches)
- Recycled round tablecloth, 62"–64" diameter (for inner layer)
- Remnant of lining fabric, 54" wide—2$\frac{1}{2}$ yds.
- Buttons
- Chalk
- Safety pins
- Seam ripper
- 2 30mm snaps for closing
- Sticky notes and pencil
- 4 small remnants of silk and velvet
- 3" circle of felt
- Pin back

Preparation

Using a seam ripper, remove all the paper labels that are sewn to the fabric samples.

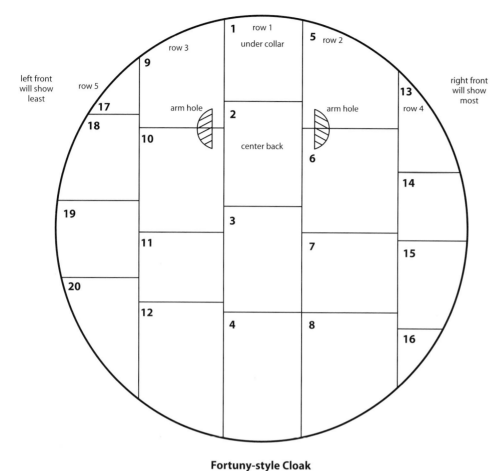

left front will show least

row 5

row 3

9

17

18

10

19

11

20

12

1 row 1
under collar

arm hole

2

center back

3

4

5 row 2

arm hole

6

7

8

13

row 4

14

15

16

right front will show most

Fortuny-style Cloak

Design

The completed cloak will be a three-layer "sandwich." The 2$\frac{1}{2}$ yards of lining fabric will be the cloak lining, the recycled round tablecloth will be the "meat" of the sandwich, and the decorator fabric samples will be the top layer of the sandwich. You will start by attaching the decorator samples to the tablecloth (the soon-to-be inner lining).

Place the tablecloth, which will become the interfacing of the cape, on a large surface and lay out the fabric panels on it. Place the fabric samples in five vertical rows, starting with the top back center of the garment. Rearrange the panels until the arrangement of colors and patterns pleases you. The very top of the circle will fold back to form a big collar. The right side of the garment will be what shows most from the front.

Place each panel on the tablecloth, starting at the top center of the back of the cloak—the first swatch of outer fabric will start at that point. This one required four swatch panels pinned together in portrait orientation down the center back. Start the next row immediately to the right of the center column. Place the first panel of the second column so that the top of the swatch is about halfway down the very first center swatch. Continue pinning that row all the way to the bottom. Place the third column to the left of the center column in the same manner. Go back to the right side for the fourth column, placing it next to row 2. Place the last column, row 5, on the left side of the cloak. You may have to fill in some partial spaces later, but don't worry about that now.

Sewing

Pick up each row in the order it should be stitched together. Put a sticky note on each column marking row 1 top, row 2 top, row 3 top, row 4 top, and row 5 top. Take these stacks to the sewing machine and sew each row together end to end. Be careful to keep them in order. Pin the rows to the tablecloth interfacing. Butt the rows together and zigzag them down to the tablecloth so you don't have to turn and press any seams. Adjust as needed.

Once you have the five rows sewn to the tablecloth interfacing, use chalk to mark a cut line on the panels that are too long and extend over the edge of the tablecloth. Cut those off. Use what you have cut off to fill in the rows that are too short to cover the tablecloth; sew these pieces on where needed.

Place the right side of the cloak facedown on the right side of the lining remnant. With chalk, mark where to cut the lining to fit the circular cloak. You will be short a few inches, so stitch some lining scraps to the sides of the lining to make it wide enough to be sewn to the cloak. Cut out the giant circle. Machine-stitch the lining to the circular cloak with right sides together, leaving about 10" unsewn so you can turn it right side out. Clip excess fabric from the circle, turn the cloak right side out, and stitch the opening shut. Press, then topstitch around the cloak about 1/2" in from the outer edge.

Armholes

Try on the cloak and fold back a dramatic collar. In order to mark two upright straight armholes on the cloak, determine how far down from the top of the cloak you want your armholes to be. It will be close to the horizontal line your bra makes across your back. Mark the two lines about 16" to 18" apart on either side of the center back and about 8" to 10" tall. Stitch around the two chalk lines, then cut them open. Try the cloak on and make sure it fits properly. Draw a slightly bowed shape on either side of the straight-line armholes. Stitch around the new bowed shape, and then zigzag-stitch along the line. Cut the armholes open.

Make 2 1/2" bias tape from the lining remnant. You will need enough to go around both armholes, which will be about 52" to 56" of bias tape. Press under both outside edges of the bias tape, then press the tape in half again, which will result in double-fold bias tape. Lay the outside edge of the bias tape over the outside edge of the armhole right side up, pin, and then stitch it in place. Turn the bias tape to the inside of the cloak and pin, then hand-stitch it in place.

Closure

Try the cloak on and decide where the inside closure should be; mark that spot on both sides with safety pins. Stitch half the snap to the inside right of the cloak and the other half to the outside left of the cloak.

Next, mark with safety pins where the outside closure should be—one on the inside right bodice of the cloak and the other on the outside left at the bodice. Sew the snaps in place.

Embellishment

Sew a button in each of the grommet holes in the fabric samples. Use buttons that are similar to the color of the fabric where the grommet is but very slightly larger than the grommet hole. Sewing the buttons on will also tack the outer layer of the cloak to the cloak lining.

GROMMET CAUTION ✳ Each of my samples had two big shiny brass grommets in it. I just worked around them when I placed the panels on the base tablecloth. Later I went back and sewed a button in each grommet hole in order to prevent the white tablecloth showing through. I chose buttons slightly larger than the grommet holes so that the button not only camouflaged the white inner core, but also tacked the outer shell to the lining of the cloak.

Closure

Make a giant scrap dragon to provide the perfect closure for this dramatic cloak. See page 12 for directions on making a scrap dragon. For this one I used gold silk, red and gold silk tapestry, and two different shades of rust/red velvet. Sew it right on the front of the cloak, over the snap.

Tips

• Lightweight silk would make the perfect lining for this project. I used heavy brocade because that is what I had in my recycle stash, but it made the cape heavy.
• Turn the entire cloak on the diagonal before cutting the armholes to get a whole new look.
• Simple cigarette pants and a silk top make a perfect buffer for this outrageous cloak.

CHAPTER 7

Upcycling Lingerie

Ooh la la! Who could have imagined we could make actual wearable clothing from ladies' undies? What fun—and what a sense of accomplishment to express your inner Victoria's Secret by upcycling lingerie! From special-occasion frocks to kooky corsets, you can make great stuff. Sew along and see what happens.

Knee High to *Downton Abbey*

Do you love the beautiful costumes on *Downton Abbey*? What a beautiful period drama. Those Edwardian frocks were so fetching—why not just create your own from nothing? Raid granny's closet for her old pantyhose and knee-high stockings or use the stash of brand-new ones in your lingerie chest to form the base skirt of this dress. Knee-highs and pantyhose? You have got to be kidding. Nope. Honest and true—this charmer's skirt is nothing but pantyhose and knee-highs.

Materials

- Sack of knee-high stockings
- 2–4 pairs of pantyhose
- Vintage Edwardian lace collar
- 2 crochet panel dresser scarves, approximately 10" x 15"
- 2 smaller dresser scarves or antimacassars, approximately 6" x 8"–13"
- Lace camisole (this one was lined)
- Small crocheted or lace circle, approximately 3"
- Lace seam tape in creams and browns
- Felt circle 3" in diameter
- Button
- Silky ribbon
- Needle and thread

Preparation and Sewing

Skirt

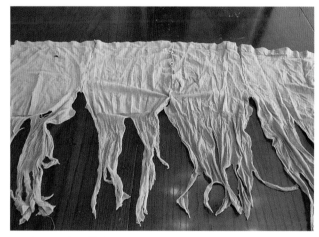

Wash and dry all the knee-highs and pantyhose. Cut apart two to four pairs of pantyhose along the back seam and all the way down the leg. Depending on your size, you will need about one to two sets of two pairs of sewn-together pantyhose. Lay down the first set on a flat surface.

Slightly overlap each pair over the last and stitch them together. Do another set if your hips need more. Make sure those two to four opened pairs, when sewn together, will fit around your waist and hips with plenty of spare room. This skirt of pantyhose will serve as the base of the frock's skirt.

Cut apart several pairs of knee-high hose so that they are no longer double but are now a single layer with two "legs" dangling. Overlap the tops of them side-by-side slightly, and then sew them together to form a string or banner of about eight single-thickness knee-high stockings. Since few of the knee-highs are exactly the same color, alternate shades as you sew them together in strings. These strings of eight single stockings will have sixteen dangling leg shapes because you have cut them apart up to the elastic tops. Continue making these chains of single-layer knee-highs until you have enough strings to make about six layers. Use the longer knee-highs on the lower layers of the skirt and the shorter ones on the upper layers.

Sew the tiers of the skirt—the strings of knee-highs—to the base layer of pantyhose. The first tier is sewn on about 2" to 3" above the place on the pantyhose where the opaque panty section starts. Each following layer is sewn about 2" above the last until you reach the waistband of the pantyhose base.

Lay out the skirt and make sure there are no "bald" spots. If there are, tuck in some single knee-highs and tack them down. Sew your tiered skirt together and disguise the seam with a few more single knee-highs.

Pin, then sew the skirt to the lining of the camisole bodice by placing the skirt on top of the lining and stitching together. Next, pull the lacy overlayer of the camisole and pin it to the lining just above the seam where the skirt meets the lining. Topstitch the lacy top to the bodice lining.

Lay out each of the larger dresser scarves horizontally on top of the skirt to form Bo-Peep–like panniers on either side of the center front and center back. Pin, then sew the two dresser scarves to the skirt.

Bodice

Fit the antique collar over the camisole front, pin it in place, and sew it down with a long basting stitch on the sewing machine. Slightly gather one end of each of the two smaller dresser scarves or antimacassars and sew them to the ends of the lace collar. They will serve as the back straps of the frock. Try on the dress, determine where the back straps (the small dresser scarves) should join the camisole, and pin them in place. Sew the ends of the straps to the bodice back.

Embellishment

Make a small round doily flower from a round crocheted or lace circle by pinching it in the middle and tacking it. Cut several strips of seam tape lace about 18" to 28" long. Rip some of them in half lengthwise to make them more ethereal. Lay out the strips in a pile, find a common center, then pick them up and tie a knot at the center. Tack the knot down at the center front of the skirt where the two dresser scarves meet. Tack the little lace flower down over the knot.

For the center back of the dress, make a hosey-posy from a small circle of felt, some stocking remnants, a button, and some silky ribbon. Each of the two leaves is made from the crotch of a pair of pantyhose. See pages 11 and 12 for instructions on making the round doily flower and the hosey-posy flower.

Tips

- If your lace is tatty, mend it before you start putting the dress together.
- Spray-starch and press your lace before using it—it will give it more body and make it easier to work with.

Bubble Bride

Do you remember Kate Middleton's second wedding dress? The one she wore for the reception? Bet it cost more than $25! This little bubble bride is the cross between $12's worth of tulle, a $4.99 skirt on sale for $2.50, a $2.99 lace corset, bling that cost $1.99, and a lace jacket I picked up for $1.99. Crisscross applesauce, shut my mouth! Couldn't you snuggle your honey close and dance to *Isn't She Lovely* in this little number?

Materials

- White or off-white drop-waist skirt (with lining)
- White lace corset
- Iron-on interfacing (if the corset is too transparent for you)
- White grosgrain ribbon, 1¹/₂" wide—1¹/₂ yds.
- Assorted white ribbons—different widths and lengths
- Sewing machine with ruffler attachment
- White or ivory tulle, 103" wide—7 yds.
- Strip of bling for sash
- Needle and thread

Preparation

Wash and air-dry the corset and lace jacket. They will be used just as they are. Wash, dry, and press the skirt.

Sewing

Drop-waist Section of Skirt

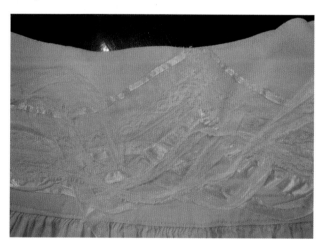

Collect a pile of white ribbons and laces of all different widths and lengths. Stitch them down as you would draw waves in an ocean—one here, one there, in a slightly wavy pattern. You will cover the drop-waist section of the skirt with these shiny, silky, lacy trims so that it looks richly embellished and not like a plain white cotton skirt.

Lower Skirt

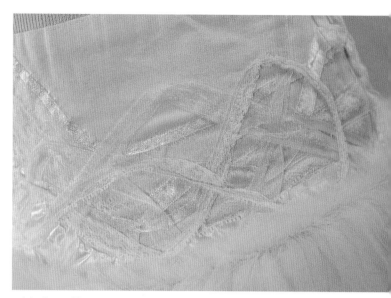

With the ruffler attachment on your machine, practice ruffling on some spare tulle. When you feel confident, begin ruffling your tulle. Both of the lengthwise edges of the tulle will need to be ruffled.

Next, begin sewing the edge of the ruffled tulle to the bottom edge of the torso/waist section of the drop-waist skirt. Start at the side zipper and sew all the way around the skirt. Cut a small slit in the tulle where the zipper is, then continue sewing the ruffled tulle around the drop-waist section for a second and third time. Now you have three layers of tulle attached to the top section of the skirt.

Put the skirt on a dress form or hanger and pin the bottom ruffled edge of the tulle to the skirt lining. (If you have a dress form or a live model, it will be easier to put the skirt on the mannequin or model and sit on the floor to do this part.) There will be about three layers of ruffled skirts so it is tricky to pin them together to the lining. Take your time and make sure you have all the layers when you pin. Once all the layers are pinned, stitch the tulle to the skirt lining. Shake the skirt out so that the skirt fabric lies smoothly with the tulle over it. Finish it off by tacking down any loose ends of tulle with needle and thread.

Corset

I used the corset just as it came from the thrift shop. If the corset is too transparent for you, cut out a section of dense iron-on interfacing for each section of the corset. Carefully iron the interfacing to the underside of the corset so that it is no longer transparent. If you are okay with the lace transparency, then no modification is needed.

Embellishment

Sash

This frock needed a sash, and the sash needed a center front piece of bling. This section of bling was a neckline embellishment on a $1.99 thrift store T-shirt. I cut the embellished section off the T-shirt and sewed it to the center front of the sash. Add more bling if you like.

Jacket

This short little lace sweater/jacket was a steal at a charity shop. While Duchess Kate's reception sweater was fuzzy, this little lacy one is just as cute for $1.99. Jazz it up if you like, but I thought this one was perfect just as it was to provide the sweetness over the sassiness of the lace corset.

Hairpiece

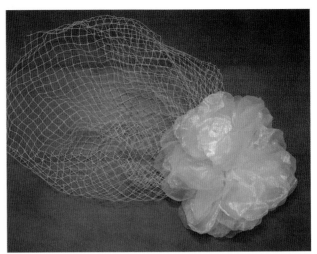

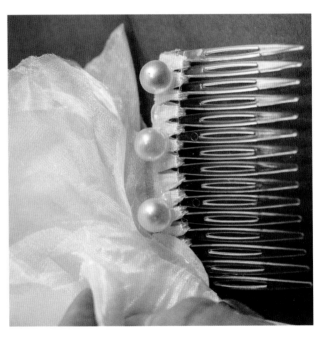

Tips

• Rhinestone costume jewelry—pins, clip-on earrings, and necklaces—are perfect for supplying the bling for the sash on this dress.

Faith, Hope, and Charity— Three Little Slip Dresses

Slip dresses are a great way to dip your toe into the upcycling game. Slips are cheap and easy to embellish. Using less dressy fabrics with the slip can produce a more casual dress, while silks, satins, and laces crank up the elegance factor.

Think of trimming up a slip as you would coloring in a coloring book or making a mosaic; just start filling in your canvas—in this case, your slip.

Slips are plentiful at charity thrift shops. Are you game to make a slip into an artwork of your own? Included here are three different versions of a simple slip dress. Choose one and give it a shot. Bet you can't upcycle just one!

Faith—Ivory Slip Dress

This vintage nylon and lace slip cost $2.99 at a local thrift
store. The rest of the dress came from the scrap bag.
This Empire-waist little slip of a dress could go just about
anywhere and make the model look like a million dollars.

Materials

- Vintage nylon and lace slip (no zipper)
- Scrap bag of ivory silks and silky fabrics
- Scraps of lace and tulle
- Remnants of lace fabric—1/4 yd. to 1/3 yd. lengths of four different laces

Preparation

Try the slip on to make sure it fits, and then wash it. Select three or four lace remnants to use as overskirts for the slip dress and cut them into large square or rectangular panels. Choose a favorite for the front panel and another favorite for the back overskirt panel. Pick out some assorted silky scraps and rip them into strips 1" to 1 1/2" wide and 3" to 14" long. These will form a beautiful stalactite edge for some of the skirt panels.

Sewing

This slip was size 38 L so it was roomy and way long. If yours is long, start by taking two deep horizontal darts in the front of the slip. Next, take two diagonal darts on either side of the center front of the slip in order to make the length taper to the back. Take a deep horizontal dart on each side of the back of the slip to continue to make the slip taper to the center back. Keep making these darts until the hemline of the slip is perfect for you. If your slip is the right length to start with, you won't need the darts.

Pin the front lace panel to the front of the slip, following the bodice line. Cover about three-quarters of the front of the slip skirt. Pin another remnant panel to the back center two-thirds to three-quarters of the slip skirt. Sew the lace panels down by turning the lace under about 1/4" and topstitching. Choose two other laces for the two side panels and stitch those in place along the Empire-waist seam line. Once you have the four lace panels in place, you are ready to embellish this frock.

Embellishment

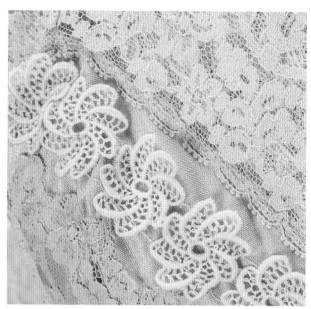

Wow, this is a fun project to embellish! Collect all your kibbles and bits of lace. You can use a lot of your tiny snips and bits in this project. The front and back panels are great places to embellish.

Lace Panels

Trim some of the raw edges of the lace panels with a variety of laces. Just overlap the lace trim strip over the raw edge of the lace panel and stitch it down. To make the shaggy fabric stalactites, use narrow wedges of a variety of sheer, lacy, and silky fabrics. Lay out your stalactites and begin pinning them to the front center lace panel edge.

Once you have them arranged to your liking, sew them down. (Be careful not to sew over the tails of their neighbors as you stitch them down.) See page 14 for instructions on making stalactites.

Silky Sashes

To make this slip more formfitting, I made sashes from scraps. Long pointy strips of cut or torn silky fabrics are the base for the sashes. Start with a bag of ivory silky scraps. You will need two 2"-wide sashes.

Start with a scrap about 2" wide and as long as you need the sash to be. These strips were about 24" long, tapered on one end. Next pick up a scrap of another ivory fabric narrower and shorter than the first strip. Lay it on the first strip and stitch right down the center of the top strip, using a random stitching pattern. Continue adding strips and sewing them down in this manner until you have covered the length of the first strip. Cover both sides of each sash if you have enough scraps. Once you have added enough strips to strengthen your sash, sew one sash to each bodice side seam.

Bodice

The bra cups of the slip are another great place to embellish. You have to go with the flow on your slip—meaning fill in the blanks where there is no lace on the slip. Cut wedges of lace and use assorted pieces of appliqué and lace to cover the basic slip fabric. Sew some assorted silk strips under the bra cups to make an underline effect under the cups. Extend these around to meet up at the side seams with the sashes. Make a tulle rose with silky leaves for the center front embellishment. See pages 17 and 15 for directions on making tulle roses and silky leaves.

Tips

- Use clothespins to hold together some of your torn strips to keep them handy as you design and sew. Clip bunches of strips in groups by length to a piece of cardboard to help the design process stay organized.
- A lace T-shirt under any of these slip dresses is perfect for providing warmth and more modesty.

Hope—White Slip Dress

This silk taffeta slip was from the '50s and had a side zipper. A side zipper allows the slip to be a more formfitting dress than the usual over-the-head slip. The silk taffeta also gave the slip more body and allowed me to use some heavier cotton lace and crochet pieces on it.

Materials

- Lace remnant, 39" x 48"
- 3-piece crocheted dresser set or antimacassar set
- 4 round embroidered linen doilies (16", 12", 9", and 6" diameters)
- Corner of a hankie or napkin for a pocket
- Assorted pieces of lace, eyelet, and torn strips of silk and linen fabrics
- Tulle
- Buttons
- Sew-on hook and loop tape, 3"

Preparation

Wash, dry, and press your linens and the slip. Once your redesign is complete, you may want to wash and press your dress again, as it gets a little roughed up in the design process.

Sewing

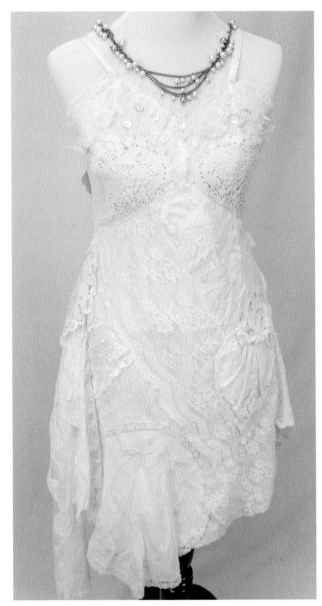

Think of your slip as a canvas. You are going to cover just about every square inch of the canvas with some kind of lace, trim, fabric strip, or doily. Start by pinning a wide piece of lace on the diagonal from under the left breast to the hem of right front of the dress. Stitch down both edges of this strip. Continue to add strips to the left of the first piece. Next, pin and stitch some strips on the diagonal from the center front to the lower left hem of the dress. Nestle the ends of these pieces against the original lace strip. Place some round doilies and linen circles wherever they please you on the front of the slip. This project has a larger linen doily on the lower right of the dress and a smaller eyelet one on the left front hip bone.

Use the two smaller crochet pieces from the dresser set to cover the front bodice. Fiddle with the crochet piece until it covers the cup area of the right bodice and let it angle down and around to the back of the bodice. After you pin that in place, stitch it down. Do the same with the left bodice area but do not stitch it down over the zipper. Sew one side of two 1¹⁄₂" strips of hook and loop tape to the crochet piece. Sew the other side of the tape to the slip bodice so that the crocheted lace can be attached to the bodice once the zipper is zipped.

Turn to the back of the dress and repeat the process.

The larger crochet piece should be pinned across the top of the back bodice. Stitch that down on the sewing machine, and then stitch a line of basting stitches about 1" to 2" above the bottom of the back bodice crochet piece. Pull the basting stitches to gather in the fullness of the crochet piece and tack that gathered section to the back center waist of the slip.

Embellishment

Pocket

Use half of an embroidered luncheon napkin for a pocket. Cut the napkin in half on the diagonal, fold under a 1/4" hem on the raw edge, and press. Fold over another 1/4", press, and sew the hem. Run basting stitches down about 1" in from the hem you just sewed. Pull the basting stitches to gather the diagonal edge. Pin the pocket on the dress and stitch it down.

Princess Diana Flourish

Remember that killer black dress Princess Diana wore just after her divorce? The one with the flourish of black chiffon on her right hip? Take a rectangular remnant of white lace and fold it over in an uneven diagonal. Pin it to the side of your dress just where you want it and stitch it in place.

Bodice Enhancement

The upper bodice of this slip needed more interest. I made tulle whimsies to sew to the bodice. See page 17 for directions for making them. The back bodice enhancement is a trio of silky, lacy, pearly flowers. Directions for these flowers are on page 14.

Tulle Whimsies

Cut an 18" section from the roll of tulle. Fold it in half again and again and again. Cut the folds so that you have a stack of little squares of tulle. Light a candle, and with a pair of tweezers hold each little square of tulle over the heat from the flame. Don't put it in the flame; just put it above the flame. The heat will cause the tulle to roll up around the edges and melt in spots. Tack these down in bald spots of the bodice.

Tips

• You can't go wrong upcycling slips! Let your creativity loose!

Charity—Gossamer Slip Dress

This charmer was created in an effort to upcycle the little bit of leftover embroidered bridal tulle that was used for the center bodice panel on the upcycled duvet bride's dress in Chapter 8. What to do with such a tiny piece of beaded tulle? Well, put it over a nylon slip, of course!

This beaded piece of tulle started life as a long rectangle with one wedge-shaped corset panel missing from it. One end of it was 36" wide, but the other end was only 34" wide, due to the missing wedge. Solution? Use a smaller beaded section for the skirt front and a larger, unbeaded section for the skirt back.

Materials

- Nylon slip
- Remnant of beaded tulle—1 yd.
- Narrow beaded-edge lace—$1/3$ yd.
- Camisole
- Remnant of silky fabric

Preparation

Wash and dry the slip. Fold the beaded tulle in half, with the finished embroidered edges together, and the fold on the other end. Cut the panel in half along the folded edge.

Sewing

With right sides together, stitch up the two side seams (raw edges) of the beaded tulle to the unbeaded tulle and zigzag the edges of the seams. Turn the tulle skirt right side out and run two rows of basting stitches along the raw edge. Pull the threads to gather the skirt so that it will fit the bodice. Pin the back section of the gathered tulle to the back waistline of the slip. Pin the front of the tulle to the front waistline, following the upward curve under the bustline. Stitch the tulle skirt to the slip. Trim off the excess tulle above the waistline.

Cut a strip of silky fabric to attach to the shirttail of the under-camisole. Sew the strip to the bottom edge of the camisole. This makes the camisole into a slip for the slip dress.

Embellishment

Pin, and then sew the beaded-edge lace over the back section of the tulle skirt to cover the stitching where the tulle is sewn to the slip. This beaded tulle is so beautiful it really doesn't need more embellishment.

Tips

- Next time you see a bolt of lightweight ivory, beige, or white fabric at a garage sale for $3, buy that puppy! It can be your go-to lining fabric.

CHAPTER 8

Upcycling Vintage Linens

There are so many beautiful vintage linens out there, languishing in drawers and cupboards. The great old ladylike embroidered tablecloths, hand-crocheted doilies, and colorful hankies can have a second life in your hands. Believe it or not the bride could get married in a gorgeous one-of-a-kind wedding dress made from a no-longer-used duvet cover. Few things are more fun than upcycling vintage linens! Play along and have some vintage fun.

Violet Doily Delight

Crocheting was a hot hobby back in great-granny's day. Every antique mall in America has booths with vintage crocheted doilies in them squealing to go home with you. But what can they be used for? How about a one-of-a-kind showstopper doily delight with corset back and dog leash lacing?

Materials

- Large round doily for center front
- 10 to 12 assorted round smaller doilies
- Small dresser scarf for center back
- Camisole
- Dog leash
- Ribbon—1" wide by 18"–24" long for corset lacing loops
- Button

Preparation

This woven cotton camisole had a back center seam so I cut that seam apart. If you do not have a center back seam on your camisole, you can cut open a side seam. Lay out the camisole on a flat surface and begin arranging the doilies you have collected. Once the doilies are arranged the way you like them, pin them to the camisole.

Sewing

Sew around each doily, keeping the camisole flat as you stitch them down. You may need to make some pinch tucks at the top center front of the camisole in order to make the big centerpiece doily fit. Adjust as necessary. Once the doilies are sewn in place, go back and sew around some of the patterns in the doilies so that the doilies are fastened well to the camisole. Sew up the seam you opened. Place the tiny dresser scarf over the center back seam and add a doily to it.

Embellishment

To form the corset lacing loops, cut six pieces of sturdy ribbon each 2½" long. Fold them in half and zigzag-stitch the ends together several times to form loops. Place three in a vertical column about 5" on either side of the center back and about 4" apart vertically. Sew them in place.

Starting at the top, thread the dog leash through the loops, adjust it to fit, and tie it in a bow.

Make a Frankenstein flower for the center front. See page 9 for instructions on making these flowers. Stitch it down and add a tiny button to make its center.

Tips

- A small, lightweight dog leash works best. This one was a giveaway at a pet adoption celebration.
- Wear another camisole under this one for more coverage.

Green Tea

This lovely embroidered green tablecloth was from another era—an era when iced tea was served on the shady veranda with petit fours and buttery mints while time drifted by. Wake up! That is no longer a common lifestyle. Cut up that beautiful green cloth and sew it into something cool, crisp, flattering, and drop-dead gorgeous to wear on a summer day!

Materials

- Eyelet embroidered tablecloth, 44" x 63"
- Pattern for bodice
- Zipper, 4"
- Hook and eye fastener
- Lining for bodice—$\frac{1}{2}$ yd.
- Corset stays or boning, $\frac{3}{8}$"-wide featherweight—
  1$\frac{7}{8}$ yds.
- Ribbon,$\frac{3}{8}$" x waist size

Note:

I used Simplicity pattern 1606 for the bodice of this dress. I did not use a pattern for the skirt.

Preparation

I wanted the skirt of the dress to have the scalloped edge of the tablecloth for the hemline. Determine the length you want the skirt to be. I cut the skirt panel 22" long from one long side of the tablecloth. This gave me a skirt that was 22" long by 63" wide.

Spend some time laying out your bodice pattern on what is left of the tablecloth. I laid out the bodice pattern on the other 63"-long side of the tablecloth. I wanted the bodice front center panel to be symmetrical and contain the embroidered pattern I preferred, so I started there. I then placed the two front side bodice panels so they would be complementary to the center panel. Next, I placed the two center back bodice pattern pieces and followed up with the two side back panels. Make sure that each panel of the scalloped pattern on the top of the bodice meets appropriately to create the finished top of the bodice. Cut only when you are sure you have it laid out perfectly. Next, lay out and cut the lining for the bodice.

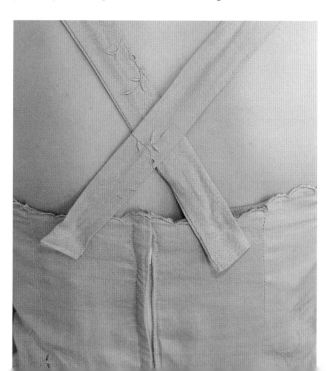

Sewing

Bodice

Sew the bodice and the bodice lining together following the directions on the pattern. Make the straps and sew them on.

Skirt

With wrong sides together, stitch the center back seam of the skirt together leaving a 6" opening for the zipper. This seam will have the scalloped edges of the tablecloth on the outside of the center back of the dress. Machine-baste two rows of stitching $\frac{1}{4}$" and $\frac{1}{2}$" in from the raw top edge of the skirt. Pull the threads to gather the skirt so that it fits the bodice.

Pin the bodice and the skirt together and sew. Press under $\frac{5}{8}$" on back opening edges. Sew in the back zipper. Sew the bodice lining to the inside waist seam. Sew the hook and eye at the upper edge of dress, above the zipper.

Embellishment

Pin, and then hand-stitch the ribbon around the waist of the dress. Make a small bow with a piece of the ribbon and tack it to the center front waist of the dress.

Tips

- After the dress is completed, wash it by hand, let it air-dry partially, and then iron it carefully while it is still damp.

Travel Skirt

The vintage '60s four-gore skirt made from picturesque fabric portraying France and its resources was too good to pass up at the thrift store. Combine it with a souvenir linen tea towel portraying vivid graphics selling Brisbane and its many attractions, and a girl has a great skirt to indulge her wanderlust. This is perfect for a "sew-a-phobe." There are only a few straight stitches in this metamorphosis.

Materials

- Vintage skirt with maps
- Souvenir linen tea towel

Preparation

Cut off the bottom half of the tea towel and save it for another project. Pin the top half of the tea towel to the skirt so that the new raw lower edge of the top half of the tea towel overlaps the bottom finished hem of the skirt. Make sure you do not close up access to the two front pockets of the skirt. Press under the edge of the new bottom of the tea towel and pin it to the hemline of the skirt. Pin the rest of the top half of the tea towel to the skirt.

Sewing

Stitch down the tea towel that you have pinned to the skirt and press it. Stitch around some of the graphics on the tea towel so that it is securely fastened to the skirt front. With small sharp scissors, cut around the design elements that you have stitched around, leaving a more organic shape.

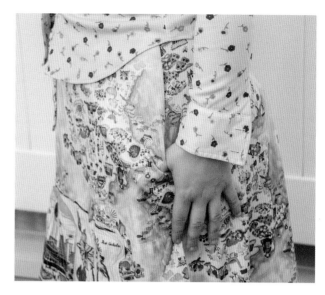

Embellishment

Adding the 1960s double-knit polyester blouse just makes this skirt come alive! No need for further embellishment.

Tips

- Try putting some lightweight double-sided iron-on interfacing under parts of the tea towel before you place it on the skirt. It will keep the design elements flat.
- If this project is too edgy for you, make it for your sister. You know which one—the scary-dresser one.

Tablecloth Dress—I'm a Little Teapot

A well-washed soft linen tablecloth from back in the day has the feel of a security blanket and the look of a trendy woman. Bet you have or can find a nice soft linen tablecloth with some cool graphic designs that will make up your favorite new dress.

Materials

- Linen tablecloth, 48" x 48"
- Dress pattern
- Crocheted hot pad
- Bias seam tape
- Vintage metal zipper
- Pearl cotton thread and needle

Preparation

Wash, dry, and iron the tablecloth before laying out the pattern on it. I used Simplicity pattern 1609. Try laying the tablecloth out flat, then folding both side edges toward the center of the cloth. That should give you enough fabric to cut out both the front and the back.

Sewing

Sew the front and back together as indicated on your pattern, then press all the seams open. Sew the shoulder seams together. Use bias seam tape to sew to the outside of the armholes and neckline. The avocado-green vintage bias tape was perfect for this vintage tablecloth. Clip the excess dress fabric, then press the tape toward the inside. Pin, and then stitch the bias tape to finish the armholes and neckline. Place the vintage metal zipper over the center back seam and pin in place. Sew the zipper in place on the outside of the dress to make a more deconstructed look than setting it in the regular way.

Zigzag-stitch the raw edge of the hem of the dress. Turn up a hem, making the dress the length that you prefer. Press and pin the hem in place, and then sew it.

Embellishment

Place the vintage hot pad on the front of the dress at the spot that is good for you to stash your smart phone. Pin, and then sew it in place using pearl cotton thread in a contrasting shade. Using the same pearl cotton thread, sew a decorative stitch down each side of the back zipper. Put on the dress and head out for some fun.

Tips

- If you want sleeves in your dress, cut a handkerchief in half diagonally, press the raw edges under twice, then pin and sew the half-hankie to the bias tape at the top of the armhole. It will hang down toward the front and back, making a sweet little cap sleeve.
- If you want a real collar on your dress, fold a large handkerchief in half vertically and cut a collar pattern from it. Use the same pattern to cut a collar lining. Sew the collar and lining together, then turn and press. Lay the collar out on the neckline, then pin and baste it in place. Use bias tape to sew around the neckline; clip the seam and press under toward the inside. Sew the tape in place and *voila*, your dress has a vintage collar.

Autumn Leaf Hankie Scarf

Scarves are one of the best accessories a woman can have. Start a fashion trend in your circle by sewing seven or eight handkerchiefs together to make your own designer scarf. You can be good to Mother Earth and a fashionista at the same time.

Materials

• 7 handkerchiefs, 4 patterned and 3 solid color
• Iron and spray starch

Preparation

Hand-wash and air-dry the hankies you plan to use. Spray-starch and press them. You may want to start with more hankies than you need so that you can audition them and choose the ones that look the best to you. Select the order that pleases you and pin the hankies together end-to-end in a long line. The hankies will probably not be perfect squares so turn them around as needed so that the end of one hankie is approximately the same length as the next one. Overlap the edges about 1/2" where you pin them together.

Sewing

Sew the hankies together, overlapping them slightly, end to end. Trim the threads and press one more time. Put down the top on the convertible—you are ready to cruise along in the breeze with the scarf flying behind you *a la* Isadora Duncan!

Tips

• Sew the ends together to make an infinity scarf if you prefer.
• Sew the scarf to lightweight fleece or an old wool muffler if you want a winter scarf of hankies.

Three-Hankie Top

Easy-peasy, fast and easy! This project is pretty simple. All you need are three hankies that you think play well together. Turn two of them on their corners for the bodice front and one on the square for the bodice back. Sew on two straps, a couple of buttons, and some little flowers, and head for the dog park.

Materials

- 3 hankies
- Rayon bias tape
- Silk flowers
- 2 buttons (shank-backed)

Preparation

Wash, dry, and press the hankies.

Sewing

Turn two of the hankies on end to make two diamond shapes. Cross one corner of one diamond over the corner of the other diamond to make a V-neck top. Stitch a square shape in the center front of the new top by stitching where the diamonds overlap.

Take the third hankie—this one had a crocheted border around it—and topstitch to the back corner of the left front bodice hankie. Keep this third hankie on the square, not turned on end. Stitch the square hankie over the pointy corner of the left front hankie section.

Put straps on your hankie top using rayon seam tape. Tie a knot in one end of the tape, pin it to the front left bodice, and stitch it in place. Run the tape over your left shoulder and pin it to the left corner of the square back hankie. Pin it in place, try it on to make sure it is correct, and then stitch it in place. Do the same with a piece of bias tape for the top right front. When you have determined the proper length, stitch it to the top right corner of the back hankie.

Make a closure for the top by forming two loops from pieces of the bias tape, each about 3" long. Sew them to the underside of the top right corner of the bodice back. Sew two shank-back buttons to the corner of the right front bodice hankie in order to form a closure for the top.

Tips

- If you need a larger top, use two hankies on the square in the back instead of just one.
- Spray-starch and iron the top when it is done for a dressy look.
- If you want a sturdier version of this vintage top, use double-faced iron-on interfacing and attach garden-variety white hankies to the three graphic ones. Now you can play sand volleyball in it!
- Wear a little camisole or tank top under this whimsy if it's too flimsy for you.

Embellishment

Make a couple of pretty little Frankenstein silk flowers to pin on where the straps attach to the front of the top. See page 9 for directions for making Frankenstein flowers.

Tuscan Rose Tunic

The beautiful cross-stitched pink and red roses on this tablecloth represent many hours of careful work by a woman many years ago. The roses were begging to be seen again, but high teas held on hand-embroidered linen tablecloths are just bygone memories. Get out your scissors, your pins, and a pattern, and you will be re-greening someone's cherished tablecloth from long ago.

Materials

- Embroidered tablecloth, 48" x 48"
- Bias tape
- Rickrack, medium
- Tunic pattern or a tunic to use as a pattern
- Ribbon, 1" wide—18" long

Preparations

This project is super simple. Hand-wash, air-dry, and press the tablecloth. Start with either a pattern or a tunic that you already own and want to reproduce. I used Simplicity pattern 1614D5 for the basic shape. Lay out the tablecloth so that you can put both the major pattern pieces (front and back) on fold lines. I did not cut out separate neck or armhole facings from the tablecloth. I used bias tape instead to finish the armholes and neckline.

Sewing

Cut out the front and the back of the tunic, pin the side and shoulder seams together, and sew and press them. Pin, then sew the bias tape to the right side of the armholes and neck opening. Trim the seams, then press the bias tape toward the inside. Pin and stitch it in place. Press under a $1/4$" hem around the bottom. Turn under again and press. Stitch this hem in place.

Embellishment

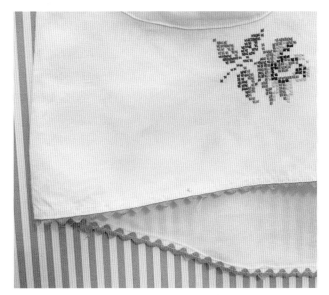

Starting at the back of the tunic, pin and sew the rickrack to the inside of the hem, leaving half the trim to peak out the bottom. Do the same around the neckline.

Cut a free-form pocket pattern from a scrap of the tablecloth that has some of the needlework on it. Turn under $1/4$", press two times across the top of the pocket, and stitch that hem in place. Turn under $1/2$" around the rest of the pocket and press in place. Run two lines of horizontal basting stitches about $1\frac{1}{2}$" below the top hem of the pocket. Pull the threads in to give the pocket some fullness. Stitch down the ribbon across the basting lines, making a tuck in the ribbon every inch or so to make the ribbon gathered. Tie a bow with the ribbon and tack it in place in the center of the pocket ribbon. Pin, then stitch the pocket in place on the front of the tunic. Put your phone in the pocket and head out to volunteer for a good cause.

Tips

- Ugly stains on your tablecloth? Ignore them—or sew a little mother-of-pearl button over each little stain.
- Is this tunic too "sweet" for your taste? If so, make it for your sister—the sweet one.

Tea Rose Topper

A beautifully hand-embroidered tiny tea tablecloth was exquisite but no longer had any practical use. The lovely faggoting at the hemline alone was worth preserving. With just a simple cut, some chalk lines, and very few seams, the tiny tea rose tablecloth became a tiny tea rose topper for a trendy girl. Engage your imagination and picture the tiny tea rose topper over white linen or maybe jeans. Nobody, but nobody, is going to have a cropped topper like yours!

Materials

- Linen tablecloth, 35" x 35"
- Bias tape
- Blouse with boat neck to use as neckline pattern
- Chalk

Preparation

Presoak the tablecloth if it has stains. Hand-wash, air-dry, and press the tablecloth. Lay out the tablecloth folded in half horizontally. Using a blouse or T-shirt that you own as a pattern, chalk a front and back neckline in the center of the tablecloth. Cut out the neck hole, then try the top on to make sure the neckline fits you. Place the wrong-side-out tablecloth back down flat with the fold at the top. On both the right and left sides of the tablecloth, make a chalk mark 2" down from the top fold. In order to make a slightly slanted shoulder seam, chalk a line from the neckline out to the chalk mark on both sides.

Sewing

Pin and stitch the angled shoulder seams. Clip the seam and press it open. Measure down each side and make another mark 9$\frac{1}{2}$" down from each shoulder seam. This is an already finished edge of the tablecloth so stitch $\frac{1}{4}$" seam allowance down each side from the 9$\frac{1}{2}$" seam mark to the bottom hem. Turn right side out and pin bias tape to the outside of the neck. Sew it in place, trim the seam, press and turn under to the wrong side, and sew the tape in place. Try it on and send a selfie to your BFF.

Tips

- This is an easy project that requires not much sewing.
- Longer and wider tablecloths can be used for this same method. They will hang longer and give a more lagenlook fashion to the top.
- A tiny silk flower or pearl button will camouflage a stain here or there.

It's the Raspberries!

In the olden days, a tablecloth was used at every meal. The '40s and '50s produced beautiful graphics on heavy cotton and linen. This square tablecloth is too high maintenance for today's living but too lovely to toss. In fact, it would be the raspberries to throw it away. All you need to duplicate this project is a 54" square tablecloth with a graphic that you love and some basic sewing skills.

Materials

- Tablecloth, 54" x 54"
- Rayon bias hem tape
- Pattern or top to use as pattern
- Tailor's chalk and yardstick
- Cocktail napkin

Preparation

Fold the tablecloth in half horizontally and lay it on a flat surface. Place the top you have chosen to use as a pattern on top of the folded tablecloth. Chalk around the neckline and the armholes on the front side. Place the yardstick under each armhole and extend it out in a slant to the bottom corner edge of the cloth. Draw the chalk lines to define your side seams. Keeping the tablecloth folded, carefully turn it over and repeat on the back side. Cut out the pieces.

Sewing

With right sides together, sew the shoulder and side seams together and press them open. Pin, then sew the bias tape to the right side of the neckline and armholes. Press and trim the seams, then fold the bias tape inside and pin in place. Stitch down the bias tape. Press.

Embellishment

The graphics on this tablecloth are so perfect they do not need embellishment. But one always needs her cell phone and keys, so a pocket is necessary. Fold the napkin with right sides together. Cut off one side to make a rectangle the size you want your pocket to be. (Make sure your phone will fit in it once it is sewn down.) With right sides together, sew the open side of this double-sided pocket, leaving a small opening to turn the pocket right side out. Pin it on the tunic in just the right spot, then stitch it down.

Tips

- No need to hem this top. The finished edges of the tablecloth form the finished edge of the top.

Recycled Duvet Bride's Dress

Memories can cost very little but provide priceless value. The going prices for wedding dresses today are $2,000, $5,000, $10,000, and up. That seems like a lot of money for a dress that will be worn once. Are you "green" enough to make an upcycled wedding dress? The process is very satisfying, the resulting dress is unique and elegant, and the price is right. You can enhance your dress with family memories and make it more special than something you could buy in the store.

Materials

- Duvet cover
- Remnants of ivory silky and lace fabrics
- White silk blouse sleeves
- Skirt pattern (I used Vogue V8858)
- Corset pattern (I used Simplicity 1910H5)
- Remnant of ivory brocade
- Remnant of beaded tulle
- Remnant for bodice lining
- Stays for corset, ½"-wide feather-weight—3¼ yds.
- Zipper, 14" ivory
- Lace hem tape in shades of ivory and beige
- Ivory 2" ribbon—3 yds.
- Large lace collar
- Lace ½"-wide tatting
- Lining for entire dress (recycle the lining of large round tablecloth)
- Fray Check™ or similar product
- Waterproof fine-point pen

Note:

Allow plenty of time for this project. It is complex and will take several weeks to complete. Don't leave it to the last minute. Harness your need for perfection—the perfection is in the love between the bride and the groom, not in the seams of this bridal gown.

Preparation

Corset Top

Cut out the corset sections from a satiny remnant with plenty of body to it. Cut out the corset lining—muslin would do fine. Do not sew the corset sections together yet, but do sew the front lining sections together and the back lining sections together. I used Simplicity 1910 pattern for the bodice.

Bodice Embellishment Strips

Rip strips to use to embellish the bodice fabric. You could use pieces of fabric from family wedding dresses, handkerchiefs, silk blouses—anything ivory and lacy or silky. I ripped strips from silk blouse sleeves and from silky remnants. Cut strips from lace and fine linen remnants also. These strips should vary from about ³⁄₈" to 1" in width and be a variety of lengths.

Memory Strips

This is the perfect time to add memories and meaning to the wedding dress. Use a waterproof permanent fine-point pen to write messages, Bible verses, poetry, family names— anything you want—on a few of the silky strips.

I reserved my memory strips for the back of the corset, but you can place them anywhere you want. Do some test strips first and press them with a steam iron to see how they behave. Mine bled, but I still liked the look so I continued on with the same pen.

Sewing
Attaching the Strips

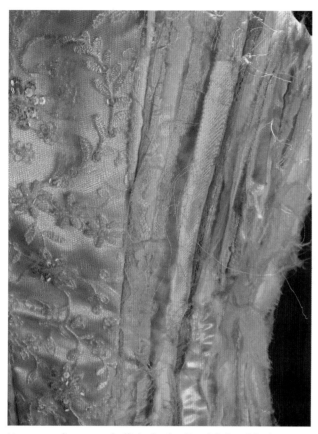

You are going to embellish the bodice fabric with these irregular strips. Leave both the front and back center panels free from this strip embellishment treatment. They will have different treatments.

Start with a side back section. Choose a strip and sew vertically down the center of the strip to attach it to the right side of the fabric. If the strip ends before the bottom of that panel, pick up another strip, slightly overlap it, and continue sewing down the new strip. Pay attention to texture and color as you choose strips. Alternate light and dark, heavy and light, embroidered and lacy and solid as you sew down the strips. When you have covered all the back panels except the center back section, start stitching the strips onto the front panels of the corset. Sew the side front bodice sections together. Use the remnant of beaded tulle to cover the center front panel, stitching it in place by hand. When you have all the embellishment strips sewn to the bodice panels, sew the front sections together and join them to the center front beaded section. Press open the seams.

Following the directions on the bodice pattern, make and sew in the loops for the corset lacing, then sew the other back bodice sections to the center back section. Following the directions on the pattern, cut and sew the corset stays into the corset lining front and back. Sew the lining front to the bodice front, clip, turn, and press. Sew the lining back to the bodice back, clip, turn, and press. Set the front and back bodice pieces aside. You will join them together later.

Upper Skirt

I used Vogue V8858 pattern for the skirt with some modifications. Cut out the upper skirt from a silk brocade upholstery remnant and the lining from a silky remnant. Sew the top of the upper skirt to the top of the upper skirt lining.

Issues

- In order to put these two different patterns together a modification has to be made. The corset pattern calls for a side zipper and the skirt requires a back zipper. The two can be merged by putting a 14"-long side zipper in once the corset and the skirt are sewn together.
- Both patterns, especially the skirt pattern, are complicated. Mark the fabric of your pattern pieces once they are cut out so you can keep track of what is what. The corset pieces are shaped similarly so be sure to mark them to keep them straight. The lower skirt panels are numerous so mark them too.

Lower Skirt
Issues

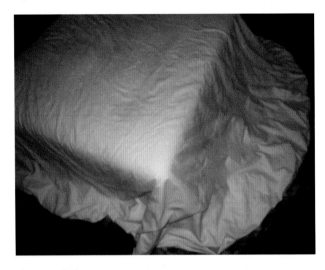

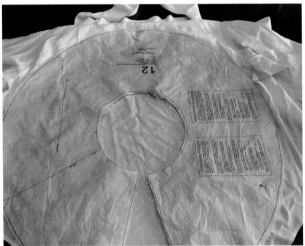

- The duvet cover that we are upcycling has two layers—the top and the back side. Use the embellished top for the skirt flounces. Use the plain back side of the duvet cover to cut the lower skirt panels.
- The pattern does not call for it, but cut a lining for the lower skirt using a discarded tablecloth or tablecloth lining. This lining will give more body and weight to the skirt, making it move like an elegant bridal gown.
- To give the flounces more pizzazz and allure, cut several times more flounces than the pattern calls for. Using odds and ends of old silk or lace blouses and remnants, cut more flounces for both the front and the back. You will stack several layers and apply them as one for each flounce.

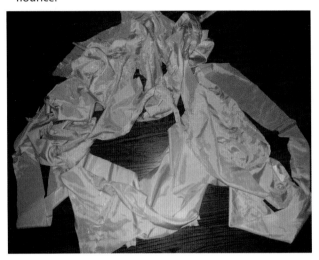

Cut out the lower skirt from the duvet cover. For the base panels of the lower skirt, use the back side or plain side of the duvet cover. You will have enough of the back side fabric to also use it for making some additional flounces. Use the embroidered top side of the duvet for the flounces and for the front, side, and back bands.

Cut additional flounces from remnants of lace, tulle, and silk. I opted not to hem the flounces on the lower skirt. I like the raw-edge look and felt the skirt had a more ethereal quality when they were left raw. Try hard to get some fabric from ancestral brides' gowns for inclusion. When you sew the two or more layers of the flounces together, keep track of which are front flounces and which are back flounces. Sew the lower skirt together following the pattern directions.

Joining the Bodice/Upper Skirt to the Lower Skirt

Pin, then sew the bodice and upper skirt front to the lower skirt front, making adjustments here to fit the height of the bride. Sew the bodice and upper skirt back to the lower skirt back and adjust for height. Once the entire front and entire back are together, sew them together completely from the top of the bodice to the skirt hem on the right side. Sew them together on the left side but leave the top of the left side seam open about 13" for the zipper. Pin, baste, and then sew the zipper in the left side of the dress.

Embellishments

Pin and hand-stitch the ½"-wide tatting just above the seam joining the lower skirt to the upper skirt. Use a vintage lace collar to embellish the upper skirt. Carefully spray-starch and iron the lace collar so that it has plenty of body. Pin it in place starting at the center back and work toward the center front. Make sure that each side is symmetrical to the other and that the lace collar extends over portions of the bodice when possible.

The corset needs a lovely satin ribbon to lace up the back. Starting at the top center, lace it through the loops and tie it at the bottom. Be sure to cut the tails on the diagonal.

Make a charming gossamer headband from scraps for the headpiece. See page 10 for directions.

Memories

There are many opportunities to enrich an upcycled wedding dress. Here, I wrote romantic, sentimental messages along with a few Bible verses. Some are hidden in the dress while others are visible if you look closely. If you would like to add hidden messages, write them on ribbon or strips of fabric and put them between the lovely outside bodice and the lining, or you could write your messages on the bodice lining. If you want, you can order ribbons that are printed with messages and include them in your dress. The handwritten messages are pretty sweet—you could invite loved ones to write them at the bridal shower. Consider using simple messages like faith, cherish, love, hope, and joy.

Tips

- Include snippets of silk and lace from mothers', grandmothers', sisters', and friends' wedding dresses.
- Don't forget to include something borrowed, something blue, and something new.
- Be sure to put a lucky sixpence in the bride's shoe!

CHAPTER 9

Upcycling Dresses

Dresses can be the workhorses of our wardrobes, but man-oh-man you can really get tired of the same old, same old. Kick a dress up a few notches and feel like a new woman—a pretty woman! The thrift shops are full of castoff cocoons that could become your latest and greatest fashion butterflies. If Scarlett could make a beautiful gown from her mama's curtains, surely we can add some flowers and lace to wake up a snore of a ready-made dress!

Not Your Granny's Needlepoint

Does your granny have a sack full of partially worked needlepoint canvases? Claim one or two right now. They make lovely centerpieces for upcycled couture pieces. This bland linen sundress got kicked up several notches once Granny's needlepoint entered the picture. Oh, and don't forget to add a nice driving glove pocket and some colorful zippers.

Materials

- Linen sundress
- Partially worked needlepoint canvas
- Zippers
  23" large red plastic
  14" beige brass jacket zipper, unhooked and
    divided into 2 parts
  8" brown
  10" dark red
  23" burgundy plastic
- Pigskin or leather glove
- Yarn and needle
- Push pins
- Board for blocking needlepoint

  Start with either a linen sundress that you like or the needlepoint canvas. Find a companion dress if you have a lovely needlepoint canvas, or if you have the dress or jumper, search until you find a needlepoint project that calls your name.

Preparations

Prepare your canvas for use by blocking it. Dampen the canvas by spritzing water on it. Using push pins, pin the needlepoint squarely to the board. Your goal is to get it to be as squared up as possible. (Most canvases are catawampus from being worked by hand.) Let it dry completely.

Sewing

Sewing the needlepoint canvas to the bodice is tricky. It is heavier and stiffer than the bodice fabric and is probably distorted in shape. Just work with it and know that it won't be perfect. Once you have blocked it and it is dry and in the shape you want it, stitch around the edges of the worked part of the canvas with a zigzag stitch to provide a finished edge. Trim the excess unworked canvas off,

leaving about ½" of canvas outside the zigzag stitching. Press under this remaining ½" of canvas. Pin the canvas to the bodice, and then machine-stitch it in place.

Embellishment

Zippers

Once you have chosen the dress and the canvas, dig through your spare zippers and choose some to radiate nicely from the bodice. Sew one 23" zipper down the center front of the dress. Sew the other 23" zipper down the center back seam of the dress. Sew the 8" and 10" zippers radiating out from either side of the center zipper. Unzip the brass jacket zipper and sew the sides radiating out from the bodice separately toward the hemline.

Pocket

Use an old pigskin or leather glove that is missing a mate for the pocket. Leave the fingers totally intact but cut the upper palm section out to make it easier to attach. Using yarn and a yarn needle, stitch the glove to the dress. Stitch straight across the center front of the glove so that the fingers dangle loosely. That makes a neat small pocket for your necessary items.

Tips

- The needlepoint canvas does not have to be completed. You just need enough to cover a partial section of the bodice.
- Use a tiny hole punch to make holes in the leather glove, if necessary.

Paris in the Rain

Have you seen paintings of Paris in the rain? Those shades of gray mist and the shiny black of the umbrellas evoke the mystery of Parisian chic. A final-sale maxi dress from a big-box store started the whole thing. It was hanging there like a big hunk of potential for $5—who could pass it by? The gray wool overvest was harvested from a totally moth-eaten Italian merino wool men's sweater and saved with the help of a skein of wool roving. The flower gave it the *la vie en rose* fashion statement. Pop open your bumbershoot—or should I say your *parapluie*—and come along. This is one fun and rewarding project.

Materials

- Knit maxi dress
- Men's wool sweater
- Heavy black T-shirt
- Wool roving
- Silky lining scraps
- Wool felting needle and sponge
- Chalk
- 3" felt circle
- 1" pin back

Preparation

Vest

Wash the sweater in hot water and dry in a hot dryer to tighten up the wool. This one had several large moth holes in it. Cut open the side seams and cut out the sleeves on the seam line. (Save the sleeves for another project.) Draw a chalk line down the vertical center front and zigzag-stitch down both sides of the chalk line. Cut down the chalk line to make the sleeveless sweater a cardigan style.

Dress

Paris in the Rain

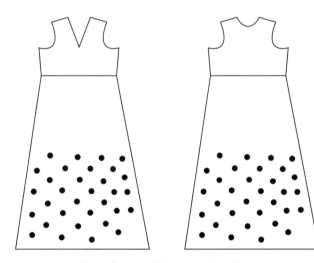

Mark the pick-ups for the skirt by turning the dress wrong-side out and making two chalk marks for each pick-up. Pin each pair of marks together.

Sewing

Dress

Tack each set of two chalk marks together for each pick-up on the wrong side of the dress. There are several pick-ups on both the front and back of the skirt. Tacking those is all the sewing that is necessary for the dress.

Vest

Cut two wedges from a heavy black T-shirt and pin them to the side seams of the vest. Stitch the wedges in place. Fold the sweater vest side seams over the T-shirt inserts and stitch them down in a box pleat under each arm. This adds fullness and swing to the vest.

Embellishment

Vest

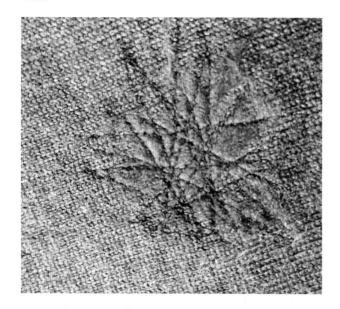

Make a lettuce hem on the edges of the vest by pulling on the edge of the vest gently while zigzag-stitching the wool roving down along the edge. Turn the vest over and sew another row of roving on the other side of the entire edge of the vest. Using the felting needle and felting sponge, needle-felt around the entire edge of the vest both right-side out and wrong-side out. This will make that lovely misty, smoky edge for the vest.

First, you need to fill all the moth holes in the vest. Place a part of the vest that has a moth hole over the felting sponge. Put 1" to 1½" snips of roving over the moth hole. Fan out the roving and make a starburst pattern with it over the hole. Punch the roving into the vest with the felting needle.

Make a large black rose for the closure on the vest. See directions for making *La Vie en Rose* on page 11.

Tips

• This gray and black lace-patterned scarf sealed the deal on this one!
• Horizontal-striped leggings with low suede boots— oh, yes!

Goodwill Hunting

This $5.99 rose stretch-lace dress at Goodwill was on sale for half price. It was missing a belt and was a little homely, but it had potential. The high-end silk camisole turned up at Goodwill several months later for $3.99. The vivid colors of the camisole perked up the granny look of the dusty-rose lace frock. The seams of the dress's gored skirt begged for the addition of a little color, and stretchy, lacy hem tape filled the order and elongated the line of the dress at the same time. The homemade trim just made the dress. It is hard to beat a $6 dress that looks like it came straight from the window at Anthropologie. Goodwill hunting is a great sport!

Materials

- Lace dress
- Silk camisole
- Lace hem tape in assorted colors and widths
- Remnant of rose cording from home décor department
- Rose ribbon, 1" wide—long enough to go around the hemline of the skirt
- Chartreuse rayon hem tape—long enough to go around the hemline
- Silky green leaf trim—long enough to go around the hemline
- Assorted parts of small silk flowers

Preparation

Upcycling this little Goodwill dress couldn't be simpler. Hand-wash and air-dry both the dress and the camisole. Choose the colors of lacy hem tape to use over the vertical seams of the gores in the dress. Start at the waist and end at the hemline. Pin them in place but cut them longer than the actual seam lengths, leaving some to tuck under at each end. Add a wider strip of lace down the center mid-line on the front and on the back.

Sewing

Using the sewing machine, straight-stitch down each edge of the lace from the waist to the hem. Tuck in about ½" at each end. Be sure not to get the lining of the dress caught up in your stitching.

Embellishment

Hemline Trim

The first trim to add to the hemline is a twisted heavy upholstery cord. It comes with a bias strip of fabric attached to it. Pin the bias strip to the outside edge of the dress hem so that the cord rests at the bottom edge of the skirt. Stitch the bias edge of the cord to the dress hem.

Next, cover the bias edge of the cord with some trim. Start with a sheer rose ribbon about 1" wide. Stitch vintage chartreuse rayon hem tape down the center of the rose ribbon, and then stitch the silky green leaf trim down the center of the chartreuse hem tape. Choose some silk flower components in the colors of your dress and trims. Tack down a little flower on the leaf trim where the vertical lace trim meets the hemline.

Camisole

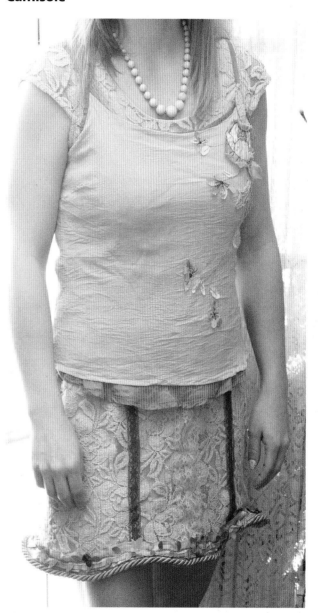

This camisole was perfect with no further embellishment.

Tips

- Don't use the whole silk flowers. Pull them apart and just use the soft, silky parts that you like.

Acknowledgments

Thanks to all my friends and family for bringing me your hand-me-downs and cashmere treasures. Thanks for all the ideas and encouragement and for being patient models and critics. I am thankful for all of you!

Alexander	Kathy
Barry	Kira
Bill	Lainie
Charlotte	Leigh Anne
Chloe	Mary
Christian	Mother
Dana	Mother Anne
Ethan	Nancy
Grandmother	Nathan
Heather	Pat
Helen	Paul
Isaac	Peg
Jack	Sara
Jim	Tatum
Karen	Trinity
Kathleen	